Elixir & Phoenix in Action

Build Scalable, Concurrent, and Real-Time Applications for the Modern Era

Jeff Cearley

Copyright Page

Table of Contents

Preface

Building modern software is no longer just about creating websites that serve static pages or handling a handful of users with a single server. Today's applications must be real-time, highly scalable, fault-tolerant, and capable of handling millions of concurrent users without breaking under pressure. Elixir and Phoenix offer a robust platform to meet these demands. Rooted in the reliability of the Erlang virtual machine (BEAM) and designed with modern developers in mind, they allow you to build systems that are not only fast but resilient.

This book is written with a single purpose: to teach you how to think, design, and build scalable, concurrent, real-time applications using Elixir and Phoenix. It is structured to guide you progressively from the foundational ideas behind Elixir's concurrency model to mastering Phoenix's real-time web capabilities. You will not just learn how to write Elixir code or spin up a Phoenix server—you will learn how to create fault-tolerant, production-quality applications that take full advantage of what the platform offers.

The goal is not to overwhelm you with theory or just walk you through tutorial projects. Instead, you will build working systems from scratch, applying concepts as you learn them, so that you leave each chapter with real, practical skills that you can immediately use in your own applications or professional projects.

About This Book

This book is structured in four major parts. The first part introduces you to the core principles that make Elixir and Phoenix unique, particularly their focus on concurrency, scalability, and fault tolerance. The second part is practical: you will build real applications using Phoenix, LiveView, Channels, and Ecto. In the third part, we move beyond building to scaling, testing, and deploying your applications to real production environments. Finally, the last part covers advanced topics, where you will explore clustering, distributed systems, APIs, GraphQL, and more.

Along the way, you will encounter real-world projects that simulate the kinds of applications you might build professionally—chat systems, collaboration tools, notification systems, and real-time interfaces.

Each chapter builds on the previous ones, but you can also jump to specific topics if you already have a background in Elixir or Phoenix and want to focus on particular areas like LiveView, Channels, or deployment.

The examples and projects included are carefully designed to be authentic. You will write real code, deal with real architectural decisions, and face real scaling concerns that go beyond typical beginner materials.

Who Should Read This Book

This book is intended for developers who want to build serious, scalable web applications. Whether you are a backend engineer looking to leverage concurrency for real-time applications, a full-stack developer eager to reduce your reliance on JavaScript for interactive features, or a systems programmer interested in the reliability promises of the BEAM, you will find value here.

Some familiarity with basic programming concepts such as functions, loops, and variables is assumed. Experience with another web framework (such as Ruby on Rails, Django, Express, or ASP.NET) will help, but it is not strictly necessary. If you have never written Elixir before, that's perfectly fine—this book will guide you step-by-step from the basics of the language to advanced topics.

If you are completely new to programming, you might want to first become familiar with general programming principles before attempting this material, as we move at a pace appropriate for developers with at least some background in coding.

Whether you come from Python, Ruby, JavaScript, Go, or any other background, you will find Elixir refreshingly modern and Phoenix remarkably fast and powerful once you get used to the functional style of programming.

How to Use This Book

You will get the most out of this book by coding along as you read. Each chapter includes practical exercises, complete projects, or smaller experiments that are designed to reinforce the concepts you are learning. Set up a development environment early on, and actively work through the examples in your own editor.

Whenever a new concept is introduced, such as OTP Supervision Trees or Phoenix Channels, you will immediately apply it through a working example. These hands-on exercises are critical. Reading alone will not make you proficient—you need to engage with the code to truly understand the power of Elixir and Phoenix.

Chapters are designed to be completed sequentially for beginners. However, if you have experience with Elixir or Phoenix already, you can selectively focus on chapters dealing with advanced topics such as real-time web communication, background jobs, or scaling strategies.

If you encounter something unfamiliar, take the time to explore the referenced documentation or additional resources suggested at the end of chapters. Elixir's official docs are among the best in the industry, and the community resources are friendly and helpful.

Remember: learning to build scalable and concurrent systems takes time. Be patient, code along, and do not hesitate to experiment beyond what is shown in the examples.

Conventions and Code Formatting

To ensure clarity and consistency throughout the book, certain conventions are used.

Elixir and Phoenix code samples are displayed in clearly formatted blocks that you can copy and paste directly into your editor. When introducing a new code snippet, I will explain it in detail, line-by-line or section-by-section, to make sure every part of it is understood, not just presented.

When talking about terminal commands, they are clearly distinguished and prefixed with a shell prompt symbol ($) where necessary. For example:

```
$ mix phx.new my_app
```

Configuration files, shell outputs, and system logs are also formatted appropriately.

Technical terms such as "process," "GenServer," "changeset," "context," and "LiveView" are defined the first time they are introduced. Wherever a concept is critical for understanding later material, additional examples or explanations are provided.

If a term from Elixir, Phoenix, or the BEAM is important, it will be emphasized the first time you encounter it, and you can always refer back to earlier chapters if needed.

Acknowledgments

Writing a book on a language and framework as dynamic and powerful as Elixir and Phoenix would not be possible without standing on the shoulders of giants. I want to extend sincere thanks to José Valim and the Elixir Core Team for creating a language that makes building resilient software not only possible but enjoyable. Chris McCord and the Phoenix Team also deserve special recognition for reimagining what a web framework can be in the real-time era.

I am also grateful to the vibrant Elixir community—those who tirelessly maintain libraries, write blog posts, create tutorials, and help newcomers in forums and chat rooms. Your generosity and commitment to excellence make learning and building with Elixir an inspiring experience.

Finally, thank you, the reader, for choosing to invest your time in this book. My hope is that it will empower you to build amazing, scalable, and real-time applications with confidence.

Chapter 1: Why Elixir, Why Phoenix?

Building software today is very different from how it used to be even a decade ago. Users now expect apps to be fast, responsive, always available, and capable of handling thousands—even millions—of simultaneous connections. Traditional web frameworks, originally designed for simpler web interactions, often struggle to meet these new demands without adding significant complexity or introducing bottlenecks.

This is where Elixir and Phoenix come in. They are not simply newer options in a crowded field of frameworks and languages. They represent a different way of thinking about scalability, concurrency, and real-time communication—problems that today's applications can no longer afford to treat as afterthoughts.

In this chapter, we'll lay a foundation for why learning Elixir and Phoenix is worth your time. We'll examine the pressures placed on modern systems, look at the unique strengths of the BEAM virtual machine, explore what makes Elixir such a developer-friendly functional language, and see why Phoenix is so much more than "just another web framework." We'll finish by discussing real-world examples where Elixir and Phoenix shine.

Demands of Modern Applications

Software development today faces pressures that are much more intense and complex than what developers encountered even a few years ago. Modern users expect applications to be responsive, always available, and capable of handling a massive amount of activity at the same time. It is no longer enough to simply serve static pages or store data reliably. Applications must now meet expectations around real-time interaction, horizontal scalability, fault tolerance, and performance under heavy load.

To fully understand why Elixir and Phoenix have gained so much relevance, it is important to first break down the key demands that modern applications must meet—and why traditional approaches often fall short.

Concurrency is at the top of the list. Concurrency refers to the ability of a system to handle many tasks at once, rather than working through them one after another. In earlier web systems, it was acceptable to handle each user request sequentially or by assigning it to a thread. But this model does not scale well. Modern applications often involve thousands or millions of users interacting at the same time, whether through submitting forms, updating dashboards, participating in live chats, or collaborating on documents. Systems need a way to manage all these activities simultaneously without creating a backlog, degrading performance, or consuming excessive resources.

Fault tolerance is equally critical. Fault tolerance means that a system can continue operating properly even if some parts fail. Users today expect applications to be available 24 hours a day, 7 days a week, with no interruptions. Hardware can fail, network connections can be unstable, and unexpected bugs can crash parts of the system. Rather than crashing the entire application when something goes wrong, a fault-tolerant system isolates failures and recovers gracefully, often without users even noticing a problem.

Low latency is another non-negotiable demand. Latency is the delay between a user's action and the system's response. In many modern applications, especially real-time systems like messaging apps, collaborative platforms, and online games, users expect responses to be nearly instant. Even delays of a few hundred milliseconds can create frustration and impact user experience. Achieving consistently low latency requires efficient system design and the ability to process large volumes of events in parallel without blocking.

Horizontal scalability is a requirement for growth. Scalability refers to the system's ability to handle increased load by adding more resources. In traditional systems, scaling often meant upgrading to bigger servers (vertical scaling), but this approach quickly reaches physical and financial limits. Horizontal scalability, on the other hand, involves adding more servers to share the load. Modern applications must be designed from the ground up to run across multiple machines, distributing tasks and data seamlessly.

Real-time interaction has become standard. Whether it is seeing new messages appear instantly in a chat app, watching live scores update during a sporting event, or collaborating on a document where changes are reflected immediately, users expect real-time behavior. Delivering real-time features requires a system capable of maintaining long-lived connections to clients (often through WebSockets) and efficiently broadcasting updates with minimal delay.

Dynamic workloads also define modern systems. Applications must be able to handle sudden spikes in traffic without collapsing. A live event, a viral post, or a flash sale can drive millions of users to an app within minutes. Systems must scale up quickly to meet demand and scale back down afterward to avoid unnecessary costs.

Traditional web frameworks and languages were often not designed with these requirements in mind. As a result, developers have had to build layers of additional infrastructure to patch these problems—adding job queues for concurrency, circuit breakers for fault tolerance, caching systems for performance, message brokers for communication, and clustering software for scalability. Each new layer adds complexity, making systems harder to develop, test, and maintain.

Elixir and Phoenix address these demands at their foundation. Rather than layering on solutions after the fact, they start from principles of concurrency, fault tolerance, low latency, and distributed computing. This design philosophy allows developers to meet the expectations of modern users without resorting to complex, fragile architectures.

Understanding these demands sets the stage for why a different approach to building applications is necessary—and why Elixir and Phoenix are uniquely positioned to help developers succeed in building the applications of today and tomorrow.

Power of the BEAM

At the core of Elixir's capabilities—and by extension, Phoenix's real-time strength—is a piece of technology called the BEAM. The BEAM is the virtual machine that executes compiled Elixir and Erlang code. Understanding what makes the BEAM special will give you a clearer sense of why Elixir applications behave differently from those built with most other languages.

The BEAM was originally created in the 1980s to solve a very specific and demanding problem: building telephone switches for telecom networks. These switches needed to manage millions of simultaneous calls, stay operational for months or even years without downtime, and recover automatically from partial system failures. Over time, the BEAM proved to be incredibly reliable for building any system that demands high concurrency, low latency, fault tolerance, and distributed operation.

Lightweight Processes

One of the defining features of the BEAM is its process model. In most operating systems, processes are heavy structures managed by the operating system kernel. Creating a new process often involves significant overhead. In the BEAM, however, processes are extremely lightweight. They are managed entirely inside the virtual machine, not by the operating system.

Each BEAM process is isolated, meaning it has its own memory and state. Processes cannot directly access each other's memory. Instead, they communicate using message passing. Messages are sent asynchronously, and the receiving process handles them at its own pace. Because of this design, BEAM systems can easily handle hundreds of thousands or even millions of concurrent processes on a single server without performance problems.

Preemptive Scheduling

Another important feature of the BEAM is its preemptive scheduling. Preemption means that the virtual machine ensures every process gets a fair share of CPU time. No single process can monopolize the system. If a process runs for too long without yielding, the BEAM will interrupt it and allow other processes to run. This guarantees that the system remains responsive, even if individual processes are slow or become stuck.

In many traditional systems, if one thread becomes blocked, it can impact the performance of the entire application. In contrast, on the BEAM, slow or malfunctioning processes are isolated and cannot bring the system down with them.

Fault Tolerance Through Process Isolation and Supervision

The BEAM treats process failures as a normal part of system operation. If a process crashes, it does not crash the entire application. Instead, processes are usually organized under supervision trees. A supervisor is a special type of process whose job is to monitor other processes. If a child process crashes, the supervisor can restart it automatically based on a defined strategy.

This model embraces the principle often described as "let it crash," which means that rather than writing defensive code to catch every possible error, you allow processes to fail fast and recover quickly under supervision. This approach simplifies code, reduces hidden bugs, and leads to systems that can heal themselves without human intervention.

Distributed Systems Built-In

Another area where the BEAM excels is distributed computing. Distributed computing means that multiple nodes (machines) can work together as one logical system. In the BEAM, distributed features are built into the platform itself. Processes can communicate across nodes just as easily as they communicate within a single node.

The BEAM takes care of the hard problems of distributed messaging, such as ensuring messages are delivered even across network interruptions. Developers can build highly available, geographically distributed systems without reinventing communication protocols from scratch.

Soft Real-Time Capabilities

The BEAM is often described as a "soft real-time" system. In soft real-time systems, it is acceptable for tasks to complete within predictable timeframes, but strict deadlines are not enforced as in hard real-time systems like pacemakers or industrial controllers. In practice, this means BEAM-based applications provide consistent, low-latency responses suitable for real-time chat systems, collaborative applications, and online games where user experience depends on timely updates.

Memory and Garbage Collection

Memory management in the BEAM is also designed for concurrency. Each process has its own garbage collector. Garbage collection is the process of reclaiming memory that is no longer used. Because each process manages its own memory, garbage collection pauses are tiny and localized. One process undergoing garbage collection does not affect the performance of others, unlike many traditional platforms where global garbage collection can cause noticeable pauses in the entire system.

Hot Code Upgrades

A unique feature of BEAM systems is the ability to perform hot code upgrades. This means that you can update parts of a running system without stopping it. Although hot code upgrades require careful design and planning, they allow for updating critical services without downtime, which is crucial for applications that need high availability.

The BEAM gives Elixir applications their distinctive power. By providing lightweight, isolated processes, preemptive scheduling, built-in distribution, fine-grained fault tolerance, and robust memory management, the BEAM enables developers to build highly scalable, resilient, and real-time systems without resorting to complex architectures or third-party add-ons.

This unique foundation explains why Elixir and Phoenix can offer real-time updates, massive concurrency, and fault-tolerant behavior as built-in features rather than optional enhancements.

Elixir

Elixir is a functional programming language designed to run on the BEAM virtual machine. It was created by José Valim with the goal of making it easier for developers to build scalable and maintainable applications, while still benefiting from the performance and reliability of the BEAM. Elixir brings a clean, modern syntax and a productive development experience, making it both powerful and approachable.

At its core, Elixir is a functional language. This means that functions are the primary building blocks of logic, and data is treated as immutable. Immutability refers to the idea that once a value is created, it cannot be changed. Instead of modifying existing data, new values are created based on the old ones. This reduces side effects in your code and makes it easier to understand how data flows through your application.

Because functional programming is built on this principle of immutability and pure functions (functions that always return the same output for the same input and have no side effects), it naturally leads to code that is easier to test, refactor, and reason about. In systems with many concurrent operations, such as real-time web apps, immutability also helps prevent bugs that occur due to shared state or unexpected interactions between components.

Elixir emphasizes clarity and expressiveness. Its syntax is clean and readable, borrowing many ideas from Ruby. This makes it easy for developers transitioning from other dynamic languages to get started. Pattern matching is one of the language's most powerful features. With pattern matching, you can match and extract data directly in function definitions, case statements, and control flow, leading to highly expressive and concise code.

Consider this simple example:

```
def greet(%{name: name}) do
  "Hello, #{name}!"
end
```

In this example, the function automatically matches a map that includes a :name key and binds the value to the variable name. There's no need for explicit checking or conditional logic—this is built directly into the structure of the language. This feature helps reduce boilerplate and makes code easier to understand at a glance.

Another major benefit of Elixir is its use of **pipelines**, made possible by the |> operator. Pipelines allow you to chain function calls in a clear, linear flow where the output of one function becomes the input to the next. This is especially helpful when processing data step-by-step.

16

Here's a brief illustration:

```
"hello"
|> String.trim()
|> String.upcase()
|> IO.puts()
```

This example shows how a string is trimmed, then converted to uppercase, and finally printed. The result reads from top to bottom in a way that mirrors how people naturally describe processes. This style reduces nested function calls and makes transformations easy to follow.

Elixir also promotes **concurrent programming** as a first-class citizen. Thanks to the BEAM, you can create thousands or millions of lightweight processes using simple constructs like `spawn` or by working with OTP abstractions like `GenServer`. Elixir makes these concurrency tools accessible by providing well-documented and consistent interfaces, along with powerful supervision mechanisms to manage process lifecycles.

In terms of tooling, Elixir excels. It comes with a built-in build tool called Mix, which helps manage projects, dependencies, testing, and more. Hex, the package manager, provides access to a growing ecosystem of libraries maintained by a vibrant and helpful community. The interactive shell `IEx` lets you run Elixir code in real-time, experiment with ideas, and inspect the state of your application during development.

For teams and individual developers, Elixir encourages readability, maintainability, and a strong culture of test-driven development. With built-in support for unit testing through the `ExUnit` testing framework, writing tests is part of the standard workflow, not an afterthought.

To summarize, Elixir combines the raw power and concurrency of the BEAM with a syntax and design philosophy focused on simplicity, correctness, and developer experience. It enables you to write expressive, maintainable code while building scalable applications capable of handling modern system demands. Whether you're writing a simple service or a complex real-time application, Elixir gives you the tools to do so with confidence and clarity.

In the next section, we'll explore Phoenix—Elixir's web framework—which builds on these language features to provide a fast, real-time capable, and production-grade platform for web development.

Phoenix: Real-Time Web at Scale

Phoenix is a web development framework built specifically for Elixir. It was created to help developers build fast, scalable, and maintainable applications that can handle real-time communication and high concurrency with ease. Unlike many traditional frameworks, Phoenix is designed from the beginning to take full advantage of the BEAM virtual machine's strengths—namely, massive concurrency, fault tolerance, and distributed operation.

At its core, Phoenix provides a set of tools and conventions for building web applications. It follows the familiar Model-View-Controller (MVC) pattern, which helps organize application code into clear and logical layers. You write controllers to handle requests, views to format responses, and templates to present HTML to users. If you've used other web frameworks like Ruby on Rails or ASP.NET, many of these concepts will feel familiar. But Phoenix goes well beyond basic request-response cycles.

One of the standout features of Phoenix is its native support for **real-time web communication**. Traditional web applications rely on HTTP, where a client must initiate every request. This model works for many use cases but is not efficient for scenarios like live chat, collaborative editing, or instant notifications. Phoenix solves this by supporting **WebSockets** and **Phoenix Channels**.

A WebSocket is a persistent connection between a client and a server that allows for two-way communication. Once established, data can flow in either direction without the overhead of repeatedly opening and closing new HTTP connections. Phoenix makes working with WebSockets straightforward by introducing the concept of Channels.

A **Phoenix Channel** is a layer built on top of WebSockets that makes it easy to manage real-time communication. Channels use topics to group clients with shared interests. For example, in a chat application, you might have a topic like `"room:123"` where all clients interested in

18

room 123 can receive and send messages. You define events and handle them with simple callback functions in your server code. This model supports not only chat but multiplayer games, live dashboards, collaborative tools, and more.

Phoenix also includes **Presence**, a built-in module that lets you track who is online and what they're doing in real time. Presence is especially useful in applications where users need to see live updates about who is connected, such as in messaging apps or live support tools. It scales well across distributed systems and provides reliable state tracking without requiring external services.

Another major innovation in Phoenix is **LiveView**. LiveView allows developers to build rich, interactive, real-time interfaces without writing complex front-end JavaScript. With LiveView, the state of the UI is managed on the server. When a user interacts with a page, events are sent over a WebSocket connection to the server, which updates the UI and sends the changes back to the browser. Because only the changed parts of the page are sent over the wire, LiveView is efficient and fast.

This approach greatly simplifies front-end development. You can create dynamic features such as sortable tables, form validations, and interactive widgets without reaching for a front-end framework like React or Vue. Everything is handled in Elixir, giving you a unified codebase and a consistent development experience.

Phoenix also performs well under load. Thanks to the lightweight process model of the BEAM, a Phoenix application can handle a large number of concurrent users. It's not uncommon for Phoenix apps to support hundreds of thousands or even millions of simultaneous connections on a single machine, provided the hardware is sufficient. Benchmarks and production case studies regularly show Phoenix outperforming many mainstream web frameworks, especially in real-time scenarios.

From a developer productivity standpoint, Phoenix is highly ergonomic. It includes generators to scaffold common components, built-in support for database integration through Ecto, and powerful debugging and testing tools. Configuration is minimal, and Phoenix applications follow clear conventions that promote clean, maintainable code.

Phoenix is also flexible. If you're building an API-only application, you can generate a project without HTML templates. If you need GraphQL support, you can integrate it using Absinthe. If you're deploying to the cloud, Phoenix works well with Docker, Kubernetes, and platforms like Fly.io, Render, and Gigalixir.

Phoenix offers an efficient, real-time-first framework that makes it easy to build scalable and interactive web applications. It's fast, reliable, and well-suited to the demands of modern development. Whether you're building a messaging platform, a collaborative tool, a financial dashboard, or a highly interactive site, Phoenix provides a solid foundation with the real-time capabilities baked in—not added on as an afterthought.

Practical Use Cases

Understanding the features of Elixir and Phoenix is important, but it's just as valuable to see how those features translate into real applications. What makes a technology worth learning and using is its ability to solve real-world problems effectively. Elixir and Phoenix are not academic experiments or niche tools—they are actively used in production systems by companies around the world. These use cases show how the combination of the BEAM's concurrency model and Phoenix's real-time capabilities helps developers build fast, resilient, and scalable software.

One of the most common applications of Phoenix is in **real-time messaging systems**. Building a chat platform that handles thousands of users communicating in real time is a difficult task with most web frameworks. With Phoenix, features like WebSocket connections, broadcasting messages, and tracking presence are built in through Channels and Presence. This means developers can focus on business logic instead of low-level networking details. Applications such as live customer support, group chats, or internal messaging systems benefit directly from these capabilities.

Another area where Phoenix is widely adopted is in **collaborative software**. These are tools that allow multiple users to interact with shared content simultaneously. Think of applications like real-time document editors, whiteboards, or task management platforms where one user's changes are reflected instantly for others. Phoenix LiveView plays a major role in these cases by enabling server-rendered, real-time updates without requiring a complex front-end stack. Because state is managed on the server, it reduces the chance of data conflicts and eliminates the need for heavy synchronization logic on the client side.

Elixir is also used in **financial and transactional systems**, where fault tolerance, consistency, and availability are critical. These systems require real-time updates, high throughput, and robust error handling. The BEAM's supervision strategy allows services to recover from failures automatically, ensuring reliability in environments where uptime and correctness are non-negotiable. For example, fintech applications use Elixir to handle real-time payment processing, account updates, and fraud detection, where concurrent tasks must be managed securely and efficiently.

In **IoT (Internet of Things) platforms**, Elixir's concurrency model allows developers to manage thousands or even millions of connected devices simultaneously. Each device connection can be represented as a lightweight BEAM process, enabling efficient data collection, command handling, and monitoring. Because processes are isolated and supervised, a crash in one device's connection does not affect others, and failures can be handled gracefully. This makes Elixir a practical choice for sensor networks, smart home hubs, and industrial telemetry systems.

Gaming and multiplayer platforms also benefit from Phoenix, particularly its Channel infrastructure. In these systems, players need to see real-time updates about game state, opponent moves, and shared events. The ability to push data to clients instantly over persistent connections simplifies the implementation of turn-based games, live scoreboards, and matchmaking services. Phoenix's scalability ensures these applications remain performant as user counts grow.

Real-time dashboards and analytics systems are another example where Elixir and Phoenix stand out. These applications gather data from various sources and update interfaces as new data becomes available. LiveView enables server-driven updates of charts, tables, and metrics without polling or reloading the page. Whether used for business intelligence, system monitoring, or data visualization, this approach simplifies front-end development and keeps interfaces responsive.

Elixir is also used in **API backends**, especially those that require high throughput and concurrency. Phoenix makes it easy to build JSON APIs for mobile apps or third-party integrations. Thanks to the BEAM's process isolation, one slow request doesn't block others. When combined with tools like Absinthe for GraphQL, Phoenix can serve flexible APIs that are optimized for real-time interaction and low latency.

In media-rich applications, such as video streaming platforms or content delivery systems, Elixir's concurrency model ensures that concurrent downloads, uploads, and event notifications are handled smoothly. It allows developers to manage encoding jobs, background tasks, and user notifications without needing separate message brokers or job queues unless absolutely necessary.

Finally, large-scale platforms that require horizontal scaling—such as SaaS platforms, marketplaces, or community-driven applications—benefit from Elixir's support for distributed systems. Libraries like `libcluster` and `horde` make it easier to run multiple nodes, share workload, and coordinate application state across machines. Whether deployed in cloud environments or containerized systems, Elixir applications can scale naturally without extensive configuration.

These examples show that Elixir and Phoenix are more than capable of meeting modern application requirements. Their features address real challenges developers face in production: concurrency, real-time communication, fault tolerance, performance, and maintainability. They provide a complete set of tools for building applications that users expect to be fast, reliable, and interactive.

Chapter 2: Core Concepts of Elixir

Elixir is a language that feels different from many of the mainstream programming languages you might be familiar with. It does not organize code around objects or classes. It does not encourage mutating data in place. It does not assume that concurrency is an advanced topic to be handled only by specialists. Instead, Elixir embraces functional programming principles, immutability, lightweight concurrency, and explicit error handling as part of everyday development.

Understanding these core concepts is crucial before you begin building serious applications with Elixir. In this chapter, we'll walk through these foundations clearly and carefully. By the end, you'll not only understand how Elixir works, but why it works the way it does — and why these choices make it so powerful for building scalable and reliable systems.

Functional Programming Essentials

When you start learning Elixir, one of the first shifts you'll experience is moving from the traditional style of programming—called imperative programming—into the functional programming mindset. Functional programming isn't just a different way of writing code; it's a fundamentally different way of thinking about how programs should behave. Instead of telling the computer *how* to do something step-by-step, you focus on describing *what* should happen by composing simple, reusable functions.

At the heart of functional programming is the idea that functions should be pure. A **pure function** is one that, for the same input, will always return the same output and will not modify anything outside of itself. This means that a pure function will not rely on or change global variables, update a file, or affect the outside world in any unexpected way. When you call a pure function, you can trust it completely.

Let's start with a simple example to make this clear. Here's a pure function written in Elixir:

```
defmodule Math do
  def double(x) do
    x * 2
  end
```

```
| end                                                                    |
```

If you call `Math.double(5)`, it will always return `10`. It doesn't depend on any external state. It doesn't modify anything. It just does its job and gives you the result.

Contrast that with an impure function, which would rely on something outside its control:

```
defmodule Math do
  def double(x) do
    x * get_multiplier_from_database()
  end
end
```

In this second example, the output depends on a database call. If the database changes, or if it fails, or if it gives a different result each time, `double/1` might behave unpredictably. This tight coupling to external state introduces risk. Functional programming encourages you to keep as much of your logic pure as possible so your code stays predictable, testable, and reliable.

Another essential idea in functional programming is that **data is immutable**. In Elixir, once you assign a value to a variable, you cannot change that value. If you need a new value, you create a new variable. This idea can feel strange at first, especially if you're used to writing code that updates objects or modifies lists directly.

Here's an example:

```
name = "Alice"
new_name = String.upcase(name)

IO.puts(name)        # Outputs: Alice
IO.puts(new_name)    # Outputs: ALICE
```

After calling `String.upcase(name)`, the original `name` variable still holds "Alice." It wasn't changed. Instead, `String.upcase/1` produced a new string, and we stored it in `new_name`. This small difference changes how you write software. You stop thinking about "changing" things and start thinking about "transforming" data into new versions.

This immutability makes it incredibly safe to work with concurrency. If two processes both want to work with some data, they each have their own copy. There's no risk of one process changing the data in a way that surprises the other.

Another key feature of functional programming is **higher-order functions**. These are functions that can take other functions as arguments, or even return functions as results. This sounds complicated at first, but it's incredibly powerful. It lets you build very flexible and reusable pieces of software.

For example, here's a higher-order function in Elixir:

```
defmodule Calculator do
  def operate(a, b, func) do
    func.(a, b)
  end
end
```

You could then use it like this:

```
add = fn (x, y) -> x + y end
multiply = fn (x, y) -> x * y end

Calculator.operate(2, 3, add)      # returns 5
Calculator.operate(2, 3, multiply) # returns 6
```

Instead of hardcoding the operation, operate/3 takes a function as an argument. You can decide at runtime whether you want to add, multiply, subtract, or perform any operation you define. This kind of flexibility is difficult to achieve with traditional, rigid programming styles but is natural in functional programming.

Composition is another critical aspect. In functional programming, you often build complex functionality by composing smaller functions together. This encourages you to write small, single-purpose functions that can be combined in meaningful ways.

In Elixir, the **pipeline operator** |> makes function composition easy and readable. It passes the result of one function into the next, forming a clear and understandable chain of operations.

Look at this example:

```
"   hello world   "

|> String.trim()

|> String.upcase()

|> String.split()
```
First, the string is trimmed of whitespace. Then it's converted to uppercase. Finally, it's split into a list of words. The flow of data is obvious from top to bottom. You're not nesting function calls inside each other, which often becomes confusing.

This style of programming leads to code that is modular, where each small piece does one thing well, and you can fit those pieces together cleanly to create larger behaviors.

In real-world systems, this matters a lot. Whether you're processing incoming HTTP requests, transforming data for a database, or responding to a WebSocket message in real time, functional programming helps you build systems where data flows clearly and transformations are easy to follow.

For example, imagine building a pipeline that processes user data submitted through a form. In a functional approach, you might create a series of small functions: one that validates the input, one that sanitizes the input, one that transforms it into a database format, and one that inserts it into the database. Each function is simple. Together, they form a powerful, understandable pipeline. If one step needs to change, you can replace it without touching the others.

Functional programming also makes testing easier. Because pure functions are isolated and predictable, you can test them independently of the system as a whole. You don't need to set up complex environments or mock databases just to verify that a function adds two numbers correctly or formats a string the right way.

In larger projects, these benefits multiply. Systems built with functional principles are easier to maintain, easier to extend, and easier to debug. Instead of chasing down hidden state changes or untangling complex object hierarchies, you work with clear flows of data and predictable transformations.

By committing to functional programming in Elixir, you gain these advantages automatically. The language itself gently nudges you toward good practices, and the community provides libraries and tools that build on these ideas consistently.

Immutability and Concurrency

One of the core ideas in Elixir—and one that fundamentally shapes how you design applications—is immutability. In Elixir, every piece of data is immutable by default. This means that once you assign a value to a variable, that value cannot be changed. Instead, if you need a new value, you create a new variable that represents the updated state.

This might sound restrictive at first, especially if you're coming from languages like JavaScript, Python, or Java, where mutating variables and objects is a common practice. But once you get used to it, immutability quickly becomes a source of clarity and safety in your programs—especially when your application needs to handle many operations at the same time.

Let's walk through what immutability means in practice.

Here's a basic example in Elixir:

```
score = 10
new_score = score + 5

IO.puts("Original score: #{score}")        # Outputs:
Original score: 10
IO.puts("Updated score: #{new_score}")  # Outputs:
Updated score: 15
```

In this example, we started with a `score` of 10. When we added 5, Elixir did not change the original `score` variable. Instead, it created a new value `new_score`. The original remains untouched. That is the default behavior. There's no special syntax to make a variable immutable—because **everything is immutable**.

This small feature eliminates an entire category of bugs related to shared state and unexpected mutations. If you've ever had a function in another language accidentally modify a value that another part of your code was relying on, you'll appreciate the confidence that immutability brings.

27

Now, let's link this concept to concurrency.

When you're building modern applications, concurrency is no longer optional. You often need to run many things at the same time: handling multiple user requests, managing real-time updates, processing background jobs, or monitoring external systems. The problem is that concurrency becomes dangerous when multiple parts of a program try to change shared data at the same time.

In many languages, developers use locks, semaphores, or atomic operations to prevent two threads from modifying the same variable simultaneously. These synchronization mechanisms work, but they're hard to get right. Race conditions, deadlocks, and inconsistent state are all common problems.

Elixir avoids these problems entirely by designing concurrency around **process isolation** and **message passing**, built on top of the BEAM virtual machine. Since all data in Elixir is immutable, there's no need for locks. Processes never share memory. They each have their own isolated environment, and they communicate exclusively by sending messages to each other.

Let's look at a basic example of concurrency in Elixir using the `spawn` function:

```
spawn(fn ->

  IO.puts("Running in a separate process.")

end)
```

When you call `spawn/1`, Elixir creates a new lightweight process that runs independently. This process doesn't share any memory with the parent process. If you want to send it data, you pass it as a message.

Here's how that looks:

```
defmodule Greeter do
  def start do
    spawn(fn -> listen() end)
  end
```

```
  def listen do
    receive do
      {:greet, name} ->
        IO.puts("Hello, #{name}")
    end
  end
end

pid = Greeter.start()
send(pid, {:greet, "Ada"})
```

In this example, we start a new process that listens for a `{:greet, name}` message. When we send the message, the process responds by printing a greeting. The data sent in the message is immutable. The receiving process gets its own copy. There's no risk of shared data being accidentally modified or corrupted.

This model scales naturally. Because processes don't share memory and never modify shared state, you can run hundreds of thousands of them without needing to worry about synchronization issues. The BEAM virtual machine is optimized for exactly this kind of workload.

To understand the impact this has in real applications, think of a live messaging system. When thousands of users are sending and receiving messages at the same time, each chat connection can be modeled as a separate process. Each user's messages are handled in isolation. If one process crashes or becomes slow, it doesn't affect the others. Supervisors can automatically restart failed processes. The overall system remains responsive, robust, and scalable—all without requiring complex coordination between threads.

This is also why Elixir is such a great fit for systems that demand **real-time updates**, **low latency**, and **high availability**. Whether you're building a multiplayer game, a live dashboard, or an IoT controller that manages sensor data across thousands of devices, this model helps you scale efficiently while keeping your application reliable.

Another area where immutability shines is in **testing**. When you know that functions don't change global state and that variables don't mutate, it becomes much easier to test behavior. You can test a function in isolation, confident that it won't unexpectedly affect or depend on anything outside of its inputs. This leads to simpler tests and fewer edge cases.

Here's a short practical exercise to reinforce the idea:

Try writing a function that counts the words in a string, without mutating anything:

```
defmodule WordCounter do
  def count_words(string) do
    string
    |> String.trim()
    |> String.split()
    |> length()
  end
end


IO.puts WordCounter.count_words("  hello from
Elixir world  ")  # Outputs: 4
```

Every function in the chain returns new data. Nothing is changed in place. The original string is never modified. This is how idiomatic Elixir code behaves—clean, predictable, and safe.

The combination of **immutability** and **lightweight concurrency** through isolated processes is what gives Elixir its superpower. You can write highly parallel, reliable applications without dealing with the overhead and complexity of managing shared state manually. You get safety and scalability by default.

Processes, Message Passing, and OTP Basics

If you truly want to understand what makes Elixir so uniquely powerful for building scalable and reliable applications, you need to get comfortable with the concepts of processes and message passing. These are not optional topics tucked away in advanced sections of the language; they are fundamental to how everything works, from basic scripts to massive distributed systems. On top of this foundation sits OTP, a collection of battle-tested libraries and design patterns that help you build fault-tolerant, concurrent applications.

Let's start with the most basic building block: the process.

In Elixir, when we talk about a **process**, we don't mean an operating system process like you would find in Linux or Windows. An Elixir process is a very lightweight, independent unit of execution managed by the BEAM virtual machine. These processes are incredibly cheap to create—so cheap, in fact, that it's common to have hundreds of thousands or even millions of them running at the same time without any trouble.

Each process has its own isolated memory and state. No two processes share memory. If one process crashes, it doesn't directly affect the others. This isolation is critical for building systems that can recover gracefully from errors.

Starting a new process in Elixir is simple. Here's an example:

```
spawn(fn ->

  IO.puts("I am running in a new process")

end)
```

When you call `spawn/1`, Elixir creates a new process that runs the anonymous function you provide. This function prints a message, then exits. The parent process continues running separately. They do not block each other, and they do not share data.

Of course, real systems aren't just isolated functions—they require processes to work together. This leads us to **message passing**.

In Elixir, processes communicate by sending and receiving messages. Messages are delivered asynchronously, meaning that when you send a message, you don't wait for the recipient to process it. You simply send it and move on. The receiving process has its own mailbox where incoming messages are queued up, and it can choose when and how to respond.

Here's a simple example of message passing:

```
pid = spawn(fn ->
  receive do
    {:hello, name} -> IO.puts("Hello, #{name}")
  end
end)
```

```
send(pid, {:hello, "Elixir"})
```

First, we spawn a process that waits for a message using `receive`. When it gets a message matching the pattern {:hello, name}, it prints a greeting. Then, from the main process, we send it a message using send/2.

This message-passing approach is very powerful because it completely avoids shared memory and locking problems. Each process handles its own messages at its own pace. No process can directly interfere with another's state.

You might wonder what happens if the process never receives a message matching the expected pattern. In that case, it simply waits. It doesn't crash unless you explicitly tell it to. This model gives you a lot of control over timing and communication in your system.

Now, if you start building systems with many processes, you will quickly find that managing them manually becomes complex. How do you restart a failed process? How do you group related processes? How do you structure your application so that it can handle unexpected failures gracefully?

This is where **OTP** comes into the picture.

OTP stands for **Open Telecom Platform**—a name that reflects its roots in the telecom industry where high reliability was mandatory. In practice, OTP is a set of libraries, patterns, and tools that make it easier to build, supervise, and coordinate processes.

One of the most commonly used abstractions in OTP is the **GenServer**.

A GenServer (short for "Generic Server") is a module that abstracts the common pattern of having a process maintain state and handle requests. Instead of writing manual `receive` loops, you define a set of callback functions that OTP knows how to call.

Here's a basic example of a counter implemented with a GenServer:

```
defmodule Counter do
  use GenServer

  # Client API

  def start_link(initial_value) do
```

```elixir
    GenServer.start_link(__MODULE__, initial_value,
name: __MODULE__)
  end

  def increment do
    GenServer.call(__MODULE__, :increment)
  end

  def get_value do
    GenServer.call(__MODULE__, :get_value)
  end

  # Server Callbacks

  @impl true
  def init(initial_value) do
    {:ok, initial_value}
  end

  @impl true
  def handle_call(:increment, _from, state) do
    {:reply, :ok, state + 1}
  end

  @impl true
  def handle_call(:get_value, _from, state) do
    {:reply, state, state}
  end
end
```

Let's walk through what's happening here.

The `start_link/1` function starts a new GenServer process. The `init/1` callback initializes the state. The `handle_call/3` functions respond to synchronous calls: one increments the counter, and the other retrieves the current value. Each function receives the current state, decides what to do, and returns the updated state.

Using a GenServer gives you a clear, structured way to define long-lived processes that hold state, respond to requests, and handle messages safely.

But what if your GenServer crashes? How do you ensure that the system recovers without manual intervention?

33

That's where **Supervisors** come into play.

A Supervisor is another OTP behavior whose job is to monitor other processes. If a child process crashes, the supervisor will automatically restart it according to a predefined strategy. This approach means that you don't have to write complicated error recovery code yourself—the platform handles it for you.

Here's how you could supervise the `Counter` GenServer:

```elixir
defmodule MyApp.Supervisor do
  use Supervisor

  def start_link(_) do
    Supervisor.start_link(__MODULE__, :ok, name: __MODULE__)
  end

  @impl true
  def init(:ok) do
    children = [
      {Counter, 0}
    ]

    Supervisor.init(children, strategy: :one_for_one)
  end
end
```

This Supervisor starts the `Counter` GenServer when the application boots. If the `Counter` crashes, the supervisor will restart it automatically. The `:one_for_one` strategy means that only the crashed child will be restarted; other children (if there are any) remain untouched.

This model of building applications from small, isolated, supervised processes is what makes Elixir and the BEAM ecosystem incredibly reliable. Failure is treated as normal and expected. Instead of trying to prevent every possible crash, you focus on designing systems that recover quickly and cleanly.

In real-world applications, this translates to higher uptime, easier maintenance, and more robust behavior under load or failure conditions. Whether you're building a live chat service, a real-time multiplayer game server, an IoT control platform, or a scalable notification system, these techniques are directly applicable.

Understanding processes, message passing, and the basics of OTP isn't just an academic exercise in Elixir—it's the way you build everything, from the smallest background task to the largest distributed system.

Pattern Matching, Pipelines, and Recursion

If you want to write clear, expressive, and powerful code in Elixir, you need to be fully comfortable with three core techniques: **pattern matching**, **pipelines**, and **recursion**. These are not isolated tricks; they are foundational to how you write everyday Elixir programs. Once you master these ideas, you will be able to handle complex data, build readable transformations, and express repeated operations cleanly and safely.

Let's begin with **pattern matching** because it is one of the most important and distinctive features of Elixir.

In many languages, you check values manually using if-statements or switch-cases. In Elixir, you often let the structure of the data itself control the flow of your program. Pattern matching allows you to match and destructure data in a very natural way, directly binding variables to parts of a data structure.

Here's a simple and accurate example of pattern matching in action:

```
{first, second} = {1, 2}


IO.puts("First: #{first}")    # Outputs: First: 1
IO.puts("Second: #{second}") # Outputs: Second: 2
```

In this code, the tuple {1, 2} is matched to the pattern {first, second}. Elixir assigns 1 to first and 2 to second. No need for explicit extraction—it happens automatically and safely. If the shapes of the data and the pattern do not match, Elixir raises an error. This protects you from silently failing operations.

Pattern matching is extremely powerful when used in function heads. You can define multiple versions of a function, each matching different patterns of input.

Here's a real-world style example:

```
defmodule Greeter do
  def greet(%{name: name}) do
    "Hello, #{name}!"
  end

  def greet(_) do
    "Hello, stranger!"
  end
end

Greeter.greet(%{name: "Ada"})   # Returns: "Hello,
Ada!"
Greeter.greet(%{})              # Returns: "Hello,
stranger!"
```

The first function clause matches a map that has a :name key. If that matches, it returns a personalized greeting. If it doesn't match, the second clause catches all other cases with a generic greeting. This style of writing code keeps your logic clean and focused instead of having one giant function filled with nested conditionals.

You can even match specific values directly:

```
case {:ok, "success"} do
  {:ok, message} -> IO.puts("Success: #{message}")
  {:error, reason} -> IO.puts("Error: #{reason}")
end
```

This case statement matches different kinds of results very elegantly. Pattern matching lets your data shape your program's behavior directly.

Now, let's connect this with **pipelines**, another elegant feature of Elixir.

In many languages, you often have to nest function calls inside one another, making the flow of data hard to read. Elixir solves this problem with the pipeline operator |>, which passes the result of one function as the first argument to the next. This leads to code that reads top to bottom, step-by-step.

Take a look at this example:

```
"  Learn Elixir  "

|> String.trim()

|> String.upcase()

|> String.split()
```

Here's what happens: the string is first trimmed of whitespace, then converted to uppercase, then split into words. Instead of reading from the inside out (like nested function calls), you read from top to bottom. Each step transforms the data slightly and passes it forward.

You could write the same logic without pipelines like this:

```
String.split(String.upcase(String.trim("  Learn
Elixir  ")))
```

But it's much harder to read. Pipelines encourage you to write transformations in a clean, linear way that mirrors how people naturally think about step-by-step processes.

This becomes even more valuable in real-world applications. Whether you're processing a web request, sanitizing user input, formatting a database result, or manipulating a data structure, you often apply multiple steps to your data. Pipelines make those transformations transparent and maintainable.

You are not limited to simple transformations either. You can use pipelines with your own functions, complex data flows, and even conditionals by combining them with helper functions that return meaningful intermediate results.

Now, let's talk about **recursion**, the last important tool in this set.

Since Elixir is a functional language, it avoids traditional looping constructs like `for` or `while`. Instead, you use recursion to perform repeated actions. Recursion simply means a function calls itself with a modified input until a base condition is met.

Let's see a clean example:

```elixir
defmodule Countdown do
  def from(0) do
    IO.puts("Liftoff!")
  end

  def from(n) when n > 0 do
    IO.puts(n)
    from(n - 1)
  end
end

Countdown.from(5)
```

When you call `Countdown.from(5)`, the function prints 5, then calls itself with 4, prints 4, calls itself with 3, and so on until it reaches 0, where it prints "Liftoff!" and stops.

Each recursive call reduces the problem into a smaller version of itself until it reaches a simple case that does not need further recursion. This pattern is very powerful and shows up everywhere when processing lists, trees, streams, or any data that has a repeating structure.

Elixir (and the BEAM) optimizes certain types of recursion using **tail call optimization**. When a recursive call is the last thing a function does, the compiler can reuse the current function's memory space instead of adding a new frame to the call stack. This means properly written recursive functions can run indefinitely without blowing up memory or crashing the system.

Here's another small but practical exercise you can try:

Write a recursive function that sums all numbers in a list:

```elixir
defmodule Summer do
  def sum([]), do: 0

  def sum([head | tail]) do
    head + sum(tail)
  end
end
```

```
IO.puts Summer.sum([1, 2, 3, 4, 5]) # Outputs: 15
```

In this function, we break the list into a head and tail. We add the head to the result of recursively summing the tail. When the list is empty (`[]`), the recursion stops and returns `0`. The result is a clean, natural way to handle lists without loops or mutable counters.

When you combine **pattern matching** (to destructure data), **pipelines** (to chain transformations), and **recursion** (to express iteration), you unlock the full expressive power of Elixir. These techniques let you write programs that are not only short and readable but also robust and easy to reason about.

As you move forward, you'll find that these three skills are at the foundation of almost every application you build, from simple command-line tools to complex distributed systems.

Supervisors and Fault Tolerance

When building any real application—especially one that's meant to run continuously in production—you must prepare for failure. Things will crash. External services will go offline. Code will encounter unexpected input. Trying to eliminate all possible sources of failure is not only difficult, but often unrealistic. Elixir offers a different approach: rather than preventing failure at all costs, it encourages developers to **accept failure and recover from it gracefully**.

This mindset is embodied in one of the most important features of the Elixir ecosystem: **supervisors**.

A supervisor is a special process whose primary role is to **monitor other processes**. If any of those processes crash, the supervisor restarts them automatically. This lets you build systems that **heal themselves** when things go wrong, without manual intervention or complex error recovery logic.

This concept is made possible by the BEAM's lightweight process model and Elixir's fault-tolerant foundations, which treat process crashes not as catastrophic events, but as manageable signals. When you pair this with a well-structured supervision strategy, you gain the ability to keep your systems running reliably even in the face of failure.

39

Let's work through a simple, accurate example.

We'll begin by creating a module that holds a bit of state—something like a basic counter:

```
defmodule Counter do
  use GenServer

  def start_link(initial_value) do
    GenServer.start_link(__MODULE__, initial_value,
name: __MODULE__)
  end

  def increment do
    GenServer.call(__MODULE__, :increment)
  end

  def get_value do
    GenServer.call(__MODULE__, :get_value)
  end

  @impl true
  def init(initial_value) do
    {:ok, initial_value}
  end

  @impl true
  def handle_call(:increment, _from, state) do
    {:reply, :ok, state + 1}
  end

  @impl true
  def handle_call(:get_value, _from, state) do
    {:reply, state, state}
  end
end
```

This GenServer keeps a simple integer in its state. You can increment the value and read it back. If this process were to crash, it would disappear entirely unless we take steps to supervise it.

Now let's build a supervisor to protect it:

```elixir
defmodule MyApp.Supervisor do
  use Supervisor

  def start_link(_) do
    Supervisor.start_link(__MODULE__, :ok, name:
__MODULE__)
  end

  @impl true
  def init(:ok) do
    children = [
      {Counter, 0}
    ]

    Supervisor.init(children, strategy:
:one_for_one)
  end
end
```

In this supervisor module, we define a single child: our `Counter` GenServer. The `strategy: :one_for_one` option means that if the `Counter` process crashes, only that specific child is restarted. This is the most common strategy and works well for independent processes.

There are other supervision strategies too:

`:one_for_all` will restart all children if one of them crashes.

`:rest_for_one` restarts the failed process and every child started after it.

These strategies help you design restart behaviors based on how your processes depend on each other.

To see supervision in action, try simulating a crash:

```elixir
defmodule Counter do
  # ... existing code ...

  def crash do
    GenServer.call(__MODULE__, :crash)
  end

  @impl true
```

```
  def handle_call(:crash, _from, _state) do
    raise "Crash on purpose"
  end
end
```

Now, after your supervisor and application are running, call `Counter.crash()`. This will intentionally raise an error and cause the GenServer to terminate. But if your supervisor is running correctly, it will catch the crash and restart the process automatically.

This behavior is exactly what makes supervised systems robust. You don't need to worry about wrapping every function in `try/rescue`. If something breaks, the supervisor restarts it cleanly. The process begins fresh, re-initialized using its `init/1` callback.

In a real-world application, your supervision tree could be much more complex. For example, a Phoenix application might include supervisors for:

Web server processes (handling HTTP traffic)

PubSub processes (managing real-time broadcasting)

LiveView socket handlers (for real-time UI updates)

Ecto repository processes (database connections)

Background job workers (Oban, for scheduled or retryable tasks)

Each of these components is isolated, yet protected. If a user sends malformed data that causes one LiveView process to crash, the rest of the system stays online. The socket handler is restarted, and the user can reconnect without impacting others.

Let's talk briefly about **application supervision trees**.

When you generate a new Phoenix or Mix application, it comes with a default application module that defines a supervision tree. You'll usually find something like this in `application.ex`:

```
def start(_type, _args) do
  children = [
    MyApp.Repo,
    MyAppWeb.Endpoint
```

```
  ]

  opts = [strategy: :one_for_one, name:
MyApp.Supervisor]
  Supervisor.start_link(children, opts)
end
```

This is your root supervisor. It boots up your database connection (Repo), your web endpoint (Endpoint), and any other long-running components your application depends on.

From here, you can create nested supervisors. Each component can supervise its own children. This structure forms a **supervision tree**, with the root supervisor at the top and various branches handling specific parts of your application. If a lower-level supervisor crashes, only that branch is restarted, not the entire system.

This approach—building your application as a tree of small, supervised, isolated processes—is one of the key strengths of Elixir. It leads to systems that are resilient by default, easy to reason about, and straightforward to monitor and debug.

Now let's apply this knowledge with a small exercise.

Create a supervised worker that periodically prints a timestamp:

```
defmodule Clock do
  use GenServer

  def start_link(_) do
    GenServer.start_link(__MODULE__, :ok, name:
__MODULE__)
  end

  @impl true
  def init(:ok) do
    schedule_tick()
    {:ok, nil}
  end

  @impl true
  def handle_info(:tick, state) do
```

```
    IO.puts("Current time: #{Time.utc_now()}")
    schedule_tick()
    {:noreply, state}
  end

  defp schedule_tick do
    Process.send_after(self(), :tick, 1_000)
  end
end
```

Add this Clock module to your supervision tree. You'll now have a process that runs independently and keeps printing time every second. If it crashes for any reason, your supervisor restarts it, and it resumes ticking automatically.

This small example demonstrates how easy it is to write robust, fault-tolerant background services in Elixir. You don't need third-party libraries or complex orchestration. You rely on the BEAM, OTP, and supervision strategies to handle failure as part of your design, not as an afterthought.

As your systems grow, the ability to build processes that can crash and recover without taking others down will become one of your most valuable tools. In Elixir, fault tolerance is not a feature to be added later—it's a core principle that shapes the way you design every part of your application.

Chapter 3: Setting Up Your Development Environment

Before you build anything with Elixir and Phoenix, you need to prepare your development environment. Fortunately, Elixir's tooling is clean, mature, and well-integrated across platforms. In this chapter, we'll go through everything step-by-step—from installing the Elixir toolchain to creating and running your first Phoenix project. You'll also get familiar with IEx, Elixir's interactive shell, which will become one of your most valuable tools for learning, debugging, and experimentation.

Installing Elixir and Phoenix

Before you can build applications with Elixir and Phoenix, your machine needs the correct tools. This step is more than just getting software running—it's about setting up a reliable, consistent development environment that lets you experiment, iterate, and grow your application confidently.

To begin, you need three things: Erlang, Elixir, and the Phoenix project generator. Erlang is the foundation Elixir runs on. Elixir builds on top of it, and Phoenix builds on top of Elixir. All three work together as a tightly integrated stack.

The most reliable way to manage versions and installations—especially if you work on multiple projects—is with a version manager called `asdf`. It supports Erlang, Elixir, Node.js, and more, giving you full control over your development environment.

Start by installing `asdf`. On macOS with Homebrew:

```
brew install asdf
```

For Linux users, you can install via Git:

```
git clone https://github.com/asdf-vm/asdf.git ~/.asdf --branch
v0.13.1
```

Add the following lines to your shell profile (`.bashrc`, `.zshrc`, etc.):

```
. "$HOME/.asdf/asdf.sh"
```

```
. "$HOME/.asdf/completions/asdf.bash"
```

Restart your terminal so the changes take effect.

With `asdf` ready, add the Erlang and Elixir plugins:

```
asdf plugin add erlang

asdf plugin add elixir
```

Erlang and Elixir have strict compatibility between versions, so make sure to install compatible pairs. For instance:

```
asdf install erlang 26.2

asdf install elixir 1.16.1-otp-26
```

Once installed, set the global versions:

```
asdf global erlang 26.2

asdf global elixir 1.16.1-otp-26
```

Check that everything is working:

```
elixir -v
```

You should see output like this:

```
Erlang/OTP 26 [erts-13.2]

Elixir 1.16.1 (compiled with Erlang/OTP 26)
```
This confirms that your Elixir and Erlang environments are installed and working correctly.

Next, install the Phoenix project generator. This tool helps you scaffold new Phoenix projects quickly:

```
mix archive.install hex phx_new
```

After running this, you'll have access to the `mix phx.new` command. You can test it by running:

```
mix phx.new --version
```

Phoenix projects also rely on JavaScript tooling for managing frontend assets like JavaScript and CSS. By default, Phoenix uses `esbuild`, so you'll need Node.js installed.

With `asdf`, add the Node.js plugin and install a version:

```
asdf plugin add nodejs

asdf install nodejs 20.11.1

asdf global nodejs 20.11.1
```

Finally, Phoenix uses PostgreSQL as its default database engine. You'll need it running locally. If you're on macOS:

```
brew install postgresql

brew services start postgresql
```

To confirm PostgreSQL is running, try connecting to it from the terminal:

```
psql postgres
```

If that opens a PostgreSQL prompt, you're good to go. Press \q to quit.

If you're on Ubuntu or another Linux distribution, use your package manager:

```
sudo apt update

sudo apt install postgresql postgresql-contrib

sudo systemctl enable postgresql

sudo systemctl start postgresql
```

Now let's make sure your environment is fully integrated. Create a test project:

```
mix phx.new demo_app
```

You'll be prompted to fetch and install dependencies. When asked whether to install them now, say yes.

Once that completes, enter the project:

```
cd demo_app
```

Then create your development database:

```
mix ecto.create
```

Start the Phoenix development server:

```
mix phx.server
```

Open your browser to `http://localhost:4000`. If you see the Phoenix welcome page, your setup is working perfectly.

You've now got a fully functional development environment with Elixir, Phoenix, PostgreSQL, and Node.js—ready to build modern, scalable applications.

To summarize the setup you've completed so far:

You installed Erlang and Elixir using `asdf` for version control.

You added the Phoenix generator for creating new projects.

You installed Node.js for handling frontend assets.

You confirmed PostgreSQL is installed and running as your database backend.

You created and started your first Phoenix project locally.

From here, you're ready to build meaningful features. In the next section, we'll take a closer look at the structure Phoenix generates for you and how all the parts work together to support request handling, templating, real-time features, and more.

Overview of Phoenix Project Structure

When you generate a new Phoenix project, the framework sets up a clear, organized directory structure for you. Understanding this structure early is important because it influences how you build features, organize logic, and scale your application over time. Phoenix follows a convention-over-configuration philosophy. That means if you work within its expected patterns, you'll enjoy a smoother development experience with fewer surprises.

Let's go step-by-step through the major parts of a standard Phoenix project after running:

```
mix phx.new my_app
cd my_app
```

At the top level of the project, you'll find several key items that set the foundation.

The `mix.exs` file is where your project's metadata lives. It defines your application's name, version, dependencies, and build instructions. You'll often modify this file when you need to add new libraries. Every time you add a new dependency, you'll update `mix.exs` and then run:

```
mix deps.get
```

The `config/` directory holds configuration files that control how your application behaves. These files are split by environment:

`config/config.exs` contains general settings.

`config/dev.exs` holds settings specific to development.

`config/test.exs` is used when you run your test suite.

`config/prod.exs` configures production behavior.

For instance, database settings, endpoint URLs, and logger formats are typically found here. Configuration is centralized and environment-aware, making it easier to manage differences between development, testing, and production.

The `lib/` directory is where your application's code lives. Phoenix projects follow a two-layer organization inside `lib/`.

First, you have:

```
lib/my_app/
```

This folder contains your application's core logic—everything not directly tied to web behavior. This includes contexts, business rules, and database schemas. Contexts are modules that organize related functionality under a

49

clear API boundary. They help you avoid scattering logic across random modules.

For example, you might have:

```
lib/my_app/accounts/
```

Inside `accounts/`, you would define everything related to users: creating users, authenticating them, updating profiles, and so on.

Then you have:

```
lib/my_app_web/
```

This folder contains everything related to the web layer—controllers, views, templates, channels, LiveViews, routers, and so on. Anything that deals with HTTP, WebSockets, or rendering HTML lives here.

At the entry point of the web interface, you'll find the `router.ex` file:

```
lib/my_app_web/router.ex
```

The router defines how incoming requests are matched to controllers and actions. It's a critical part of every Phoenix app. Here's a simple example of what you'll see early on:

```
scope "/", MyAppWeb do
  pipe_through :browser

  get "/", PageController, :home
end
```

This tells Phoenix: when a GET request comes to /, call the `home` action of **PageController.**

Inside `controllers/`, you define the actions that respond to those requests. A controller is a module where each function (called an action) handles a specific route. It processes incoming data, coordinates with the application logic, and returns a response.

For example:

```
defmodule MyAppWeb.PageController do
```

```
  use MyAppWeb, :controller

  def home(conn, _params) do
    render(conn, :home)
  end
end
```

Here, `home/2` renders a template called `home.html.heex`.

Templates live inside the `templates/` directory. They are server-side rendered views of your application, written in HEEx, Phoenix's efficient templating language.

For example, the `home.html.heex` template might look like this:

```
<h1>Welcome to MyApp!</h1>

<p>Building scalable web applications with Elixir
and Phoenix.</p>
```

Views live inside `views/`. Views are optional in modern Phoenix setups, but when used, they help prepare data for rendering in templates. They are modules that act as helpers for your templates, formatting or presenting complex data in a cleaner way.

When it comes to real-time communication, Phoenix provides `channels/` and `live/`.

Inside `channels/`, you define WebSocket channels, which allow real-time communication between your server and client browsers. Channels are great for building chat systems, multiplayer games, or live dashboards.

In `live/`, you define LiveViews. LiveView is one of Phoenix's most powerful features. It allows you to build rich, interactive, real-time user interfaces without writing custom JavaScript. Instead, the server maintains a lightweight WebSocket connection to the browser and pushes updates automatically.

Static assets like CSS, JavaScript, and images live in the `assets/` directory. Modern Phoenix projects use `esbuild` and optionally `TailwindCSS` to compile and serve frontend assets. If you need to add a library like Alpine.js or configure your CSS, you'll modify files in `assets/`.

Testing is also a first-class citizen in Phoenix. The `test/` directory holds unit tests, controller tests, and integration tests. Phoenix encourages a test-driven workflow and makes it easy to set up isolated, fast-running tests out of the box.

A simple controller test might look like:

```
defmodule MyAppWeb.PageControllerTest do
  use MyAppWeb.ConnCase

  test "GET / responds with 200 OK", %{conn: conn} do
    conn = get(conn, "/")
    assert html_response(conn, 200) =~ "Welcome to MyApp!"
  end
end
```

You can run all tests with:

```
mix test
```

Phoenix also embraces interactive development. When you run `iex -S mix phx.server`, you can interact with your application live while the server is running. You can query your database, call internal functions, reload modules, and inspect state—all from the same shell.

Understanding this structure matters because as your application grows, knowing where to put code—and how to keep different layers separate— makes a huge difference in maintainability. Small apps can quickly become large ones, and by following Phoenix's conventions, you'll build systems that are easier to understand, test, scale, and debug.

Running Your First Phoenix Application

Now that your Phoenix project is set up and you understand its structure, it's time to run the application for the first time. This is an exciting step because it moves you from setting up files to actually seeing your work come alive in the browser. It's also where you start seeing the real-time capabilities and developer-friendly design of Phoenix in action.

Before you run the server, there are a few important steps to complete. These steps ensure that the database is ready, dependencies are installed, and everything is wired up correctly.

First, navigate to your project folder if you're not already inside it:

```
cd my_app
```

Every Phoenix application expects a database connection to be ready, even if you're not building a database-heavy feature yet. To set up the development database, run:

```
mix ecto.create
```

This command uses Ecto (Phoenix's database wrapper) to create the development database based on the settings found in `config/dev.exs`. By default, Phoenix configures PostgreSQL as the database engine. If your database credentials are incorrect or PostgreSQL isn't running, this step will fail. Make sure PostgreSQL is installed and started on your system.

If you see output similar to:

```
The database for MyApp.Repo has been created
```

you're good to go.

Now, it's time to start the Phoenix server:

```
mix phx.server
```

When you run this command, Phoenix compiles your project if necessary, starts all required processes (like the web server, PubSub system, and database repo), and binds the server to your local machine.

You should see log output in your terminal like:

```
[info] Running MyAppWeb.Endpoint with Cowboy using
http://0.0.0.0:4000
```

This means your application is running locally on port 4000.

Open your browser and visit:

```
http://localhost:4000
```

You'll see the Phoenix welcome page, confirming that everything is working. It's a simple page, but a lot of complex machinery is already behind it. Phoenix has started a lightweight Cowboy HTTP server, connected to your database, compiled your frontend assets, and is serving your site—all automatically.

Now that your application is running, you can start interacting with it. Let's make a small real-world change to better understand how Phoenix handles development workflows.

Open the file:

```
lib/my_app_web/controllers/page_controller.ex
```

You'll see the `PageController` defined there:

```
defmodule MyAppWeb.PageController do
  use MyAppWeb, :controller

  def home(conn, _params) do
    render(conn, :home)
  end
end
```

Let's add a simple log message:

```
def home(conn, _params) do

  IO.puts("Home page was requested")

  render(conn, :home)

end
```

Now refresh your browser. In your terminal, you'll see:

```
Home page was requested
```

This confirms that every time a user visits the homepage, the server handles the request through your controller action.

Let's take it further and edit the template.

Open:

```
lib/my_app_web/templates/page/home.html.heex
```
Change the content to:

```html
<h1>Welcome to Phoenix Development!</h1>
<p>You're running your first Phoenix application
successfully.</p>
```

Save the file and refresh your browser. You'll see the new content immediately. No need to restart the server or manually recompile anything— Phoenix's development server watches your files and recompiles them on the fly. This feature makes development fast and interactive, allowing you to focus on building rather than managing your environment.

If you need to reset the server for any reason (for example, after updating runtime configuration files), just stop it with Ctrl+C and restart it using:

```
mix phx.server
```

Another common development task is accessing your app through an interactive Elixir shell (IEx) alongside the running server. Instead of mix phx.server, you can start Phoenix in IEx mode with:

```
iex -S mix phx.server
```

Now you have a live shell where you can interact with your application's internals. For example, if you had a User schema, you could query the database directly from IEx:

```
alias MyApp.Accounts.User
alias MyApp.Repo

Repo.all(User)
```

This tight feedback loop between code, server, and live inspection makes Phoenix development particularly productive.

As you continue building your application, you'll often alternate between editing controllers, templates, LiveViews, and database schemas, refreshing your browser to see changes reflected almost instantly. Phoenix's development experience is designed to minimize friction and maximize focus.

Running your first Phoenix application is not just about seeing a welcome page—it's about understanding that the full power of Elixir's concurrency, Phoenix's real-time capabilities, and a production-grade web server are already running under the hood.

Interactive Development with IEx

One of the most powerful tools you have as an Elixir and Phoenix developer is **IEx**, the Interactive Elixir shell. IEx is not just a console where you run simple expressions; it's a live interface to your entire application while it's running. This tool makes Elixir development highly productive because it gives you immediate feedback, helps you debug problems easily, and allows you to test ideas without restarting your server or rebuilding your app.

When working with a Phoenix project, you can start IEx attached to your application by running:

```
iex -S mix phx.server
```

This command boots up your Phoenix app just like `mix phx.server`, but also opens the interactive shell. Now, while your server is running and serving pages at `http://localhost:4000`, you can execute Elixir code directly against your application's live environment.

You can think of IEx as having a conversation with your application. You can query data, inspect modules, call functions, reload code, and debug issues without shutting anything down.

Let's look at what you can do with it.

Suppose you have a context for managing users, something like this:

```
defmodule MyApp.Accounts.User do
  use Ecto.Schema

  schema "users" do
    field :email, :string
    field :name, :string

    timestamps()
  end
end
```

And a corresponding context module:

```elixir
defmodule MyApp.Accounts do
  import Ecto.Query
  alias MyApp.Repo
  alias MyApp.Accounts.User

  def list_users do
    Repo.all(User)
  end
end
```

Inside IEx, you can immediately start working with these modules.

First, alias the modules you need:

```elixir
alias MyApp.Repo
```

```elixir
alias MyApp.Accounts
```

```elixir
alias MyApp.Accounts.User
```

Now you can list users directly from the database:

```elixir
Accounts.list_users()
```

If there are no users yet, you can create one manually:

```elixir
Repo.insert!(%User{name: "Ada Lovelace", email: "ada@elixir.dev"})
```

And immediately verify:

```elixir
Accounts.list_users()
```

This ability to run live queries against your database while the server is running saves enormous amounts of time during development. You don't need to build full admin interfaces just to test that basic functionality works—you can test it directly in IEx.

You can also inspect routes at any time:

```elixir
Phoenix.Router.routes(MyAppWeb.Router)
```

This command prints all the defined routes in your application, showing the HTTP method, the path, and the controller and action handling it. If you ever wonder why a request isn't matching what you expect, this is a fast way to verify your routing setup.

Sometimes, as you're editing code, you'll want to reload modules without restarting the server. IEx gives you this ability through the `recompile/0` function.

Suppose you made changes to `User` or `Accounts`. Instead of stopping the server, you can simply type:

```
recompile()
```

IEx will recompile the changed files, and your running server will immediately reflect the updates.

You can also debug more deeply with simple inspection tools. The most basic but most used is `IO.inspect/2`. You can add it inside your controller actions, LiveView callbacks, or anywhere else you want to see what's happening:

```
IO.inspect(params, label: "Received params")
```

This prints the inspected value to the console with an optional label, helping you trace issues quickly.

In IEx itself, you can inspect any data:

```
user = Repo.get_by(User, email: "ada@elixir.dev")
IO.inspect(user)
```

Or you can pipe it into the inspect function for clearer formatting:

```
Repo.get_by(User, email: "ada@elixir.dev")
|> IO.inspect(label: "Fetched user")
```

Another great feature of IEx is helper commands built right into the shell. You can type `h` to get help:

```
h Enum
```

This shows the documentation for the `Enum` module right inside your terminal.

If you want to see what functions a module provides, use:

```
i Enum
```

This will not only list all the functions but also tell you the type of the module, its source location, and its fields if it's a struct.

Suppose you're debugging a problem and you want to introspect the structure of a term. You can call:

```
i user
```

This will tell you that `user` is a `%User{}` struct, list all its fields, and show you what module it comes from.

These features turn IEx into a dynamic documentation browser, a live query console, a code experimentation tool, and a debugging assistant—all without leaving your development environment.

For example, let's say you're testing out a feature where users can follow each other. You haven't written a user interface yet, but you want to test the data model. You can define associations in your schema, and immediately create mock users in IEx, associate them, and query them—all without touching the browser.

IEx also helps when developing LiveView applications. You can inspect the state of LiveViews, look at PubSub topics, and debug real-time interactions while your app is still serving live users. This kind of powerful introspection makes building real-time, scalable applications much less risky and much more manageable.

Interactive development with IEx is not a luxury in Elixir development—it is an expected, natural part of the workflow. Elixir's tooling assumes you will be coding, inspecting, debugging, and learning dynamically as you build your application.

By working closely with IEx, you build a deeper, more intuitive understanding of your code. You'll spot problems earlier, fix issues faster, and prototype features more confidently.

Chapter 4: Building Your First Phoenix Application

Now that your Phoenix project is running and you're comfortable working interactively with IEx, it's time to build real features into your application. In this chapter, we're going to walk through the fundamental building blocks of any Phoenix app: **routing requests**, **controllers**, **views**, **templates**, **contexts**, **domain logic**, and **database integration** through Ecto.

You'll see how each piece connects to the next. This will give you a complete workflow—from the moment a user's browser sends a request, all the way to generating a dynamic response pulled from your database. You'll be writing actual code, handling real user interactions, and beginning to structure your application properly.

Routing Requests

In every Phoenix application, routing is the first layer that receives and interprets incoming HTTP requests. It's the traffic controller that decides which controller action should respond to a particular URL and HTTP method. Routes are not just configuration—they are functions. They match patterns and hand off the connection (`conn`) object to the appropriate part of your application, triggering all the logic that follows.

Routes in Phoenix are defined in a single file:

```
lib/my_app_web/router.ex
```

When you open that file in a fresh Phoenix project, you'll find some scaffolding already in place. The file defines **pipelines** and **scopes**—two concepts that help structure and secure how requests are handled.

Pipelines

A pipeline is a sequence of Plugs. A Plug is a composable module or function that transforms the connection struct (`Plug.Conn`) before it reaches your controller. You can think of it as middleware.

Here's a typical browser pipeline in the Phoenix router:

```
pipeline :browser do
  plug :accepts, ["html"]
  plug :fetch_session
  plug :fetch_flash
  plug :protect_from_forgery
  plug :put_secure_browser_headers
end
```

This pipeline prepares the connection for handling browser-based requests. It ensures the content is HTML, sets up the session and flash (for temporary messages like notifications), protects against CSRF attacks, and sets security headers.

There's also usually an API pipeline:

```
pipeline :api do

  plug :accepts, ["json"]

end
```

This one strips things down to just what's necded for JSON-based API requests. You'll use it when building mobile backends or exposing public API endpoints.

Scopes

A scope groups routes under a common path and pipeline. It helps organize your app and apply consistent behavior.

For instance, the default scope looks like this:

```
scope "/", MyAppWeb do
  pipe_through :browser

  get "/", PageController, :home
end
```

This says: any request starting with /, go through the :browser pipeline, and treat MyAppWeb as the namespace for the controllers and views.

Now let's break down a single route:

```
get "/about", PageController, :about
```

This line defines a GET route. When a request comes in for /about, Phoenix will call the about/2 action in the PageController. The controller receives two arguments: the connection (conn) and the request parameters (params). It's then responsible for building the response.

Here's how that controller might look:

```
defmodule MyAppWeb.PageController do
  use MyAppWeb, :controller

  def about(conn, _params) do
    render(conn, :about)
  end
end
```

The render/2 function looks for a template named about.html.heex in the appropriate view folder and renders it. Phoenix follows naming conventions, so you don't need to explicitly specify the template path if your names match.

If you need to match a different method—say, a POST—you change the verb:

```
post "/contact", ContactController, :create
```

This is useful for form submissions, where the user submits data via POST and expects the server to respond based on that data.

Named Parameters and Path Matching

Phoenix allows dynamic segments in your routes. For example:

```
get "/books/:id", BookController, :show
```

If someone visits /books/42, Phoenix will route the request to BookController.show/2 and pass %{"id" => "42"} in the params map. You can access this inside your controller like:

```
def show(conn, %{"id" => id}) do
  book = Library.get_book!(id)
  render(conn, :show, book: book)
end
```

This lets you fetch records based on IDs, slugs, or any identifier present in the URL.

You can even nest parameters:

```
get "/authors/:author_id/books/:book_id",
BookController, :show
```

This route passes both `author_id` and `book_id` into the `params`, giving you access to them in the controller for building relationships or nested views.

Grouping Routes with Resources

For standard CRUD operations, Phoenix gives you a shortcut with `resources`:

```
resources "/books", BookController
```

This expands into seven routes:

GET /books → index

GET /books/new → new

POST /books → create

GET /books/:id → show

GET /books/:id/edit → edit

PUT /books/:id → update

DELETE /books/:id → delete

This is ideal when building administrative dashboards or RESTful APIs.

If you only need a subset, you can use the `only` or `except` option:

```
resources "/books", BookController, only: [:index, :show]
```

Custom Pipelines for Authentication or Admin Access

As your application grows, you'll want more control over who can access certain routes. You can create custom pipelines for things like authentication or admin roles.

For example:

```
pipeline :admin do
  plug MyAppWeb.Plugs.RequireAdmin
end

scope "/admin", MyAppWeb do
  pipe_through [:browser, :admin]

  get "/dashboard", AdminController, :index
end
```

This pattern ensures that only authenticated admin users can access anything under /admin. The RequireAdmin plug would redirect unauthorized users to a login page or show an error.

You can combine multiple pipelines, making it easy to compose access control in a readable way.

Fallback Routes

Sometimes you want to catch unmatched routes and show a 404 page. Phoenix doesn't provide a catch-all route by default, but you can handle it using a match clause and custom plug:

```
match _, "/*path", MyAppWeb.FallbackController,
:not_found
```

This should be placed last in your router, as it will match anything not caught by earlier routes.

Routing in Phoenix is straightforward, powerful, and flexible. The combination of clear syntax, powerful pattern matching, and composable pipelines gives you fine-grained control over how requests are handled. Whether you're building a traditional HTML site, a modern LiveView interface, or a JSON API for mobile clients, Phoenix routing is built to scale with you.

Controllers, Views, and Templates

Once a request reaches your Phoenix application through the router, it needs to be handled, processed, and turned into a response. That entire process typically begins in a **controller**, which may invoke some business logic, and ends by rendering content using **templates**—optionally shaped by a **view**.

These three components—controllers, views, and templates—work together to generate dynamic responses in Phoenix applications.

Controllers: Handling the Request

A controller is where your application receives incoming HTTP requests and decides how to respond. A controller is just a module that uses `Phoenix.Controller`, with one function for each "action" you want to handle.

Here's a basic controller module:

```
defmodule MyAppWeb.BookController do
  use MyAppWeb, :controller

  def index(conn, _params) do
    books = [
      %{title: "Elixir in Action", author: "Sasa
Juric"},
      %{title: "Programming Phoenix", author:
"Chris McCord"}
    ]

    render(conn, :index, books: books)
  end
end
```

In this example, the `index/2` function is an action that accepts a `conn` struct and a map of request `params`. The `conn` contains the state of the HTTP request (headers, path, session data, etc.) and will eventually carry the response back to the browser.

We hardcoded a list of books and passed it into the `render/3` function. This function tells Phoenix: render the `index.html.heex` template from the `book` view, passing it the list of books.

Each controller action typically ends with one of two outcomes: rendering a template or redirecting the client.

Templates: Presenting the Output

Templates are HTML pages with embedded Elixir expressions. Phoenix uses **HEEx (HTML + EEx)** templates, which provide both performance and safety enhancements over earlier .eex templates.

By default, templates live under:

```
lib/my_app_web/templates/
```

Following the controller example, you should create a folder named book and place an index.html.heex file inside it:

```
<!-- lib/my_app_web/templates/book/index.html.heex
-->

<h1>Books</h1>

<ul>
<%= for book <- @books do %>
  <li><%= book.title %> by <%= book.author %></li>
<% end %>
</ul>
```

This template uses <%= %> to interpolate Elixir expressions. The @books variable is automatically passed to the template from the controller via the render/3 call. You can loop over it, print values, and construct dynamic content using any Elixir logic supported in HEEx.

If you mistype a variable name, HEEx will raise a compile-time error rather than failing silently—this helps catch mistakes early.

Views: Structuring Presentation Logic

A **view** in Phoenix is a module used to encapsulate template-related logic. If templates are your HTML, then views are the helpers that format and prepare the data shown in that HTML.

By default, views live under:

```
lib/my_app_web/views/
```

Create a view for the BookController like this:

```
defmodule MyAppWeb.BookView do
```

```
  use MyAppWeb, :view

  def format_author_name(%{author: author}) do
    String.upcase(author)
  end
end
```

Now you can use `format_author_name/1` in your template:

```
<ul>
<%= for book <- @books do %>
  <li>
    <%= book.title %> by <%=
format_author_name(book) %>
  </li>
<% end %>
</ul>
```

By placing logic like string formatting or conditional presentation in the view, you keep your templates clean and free from complex logic. Views can also define fallback behavior, like formatting nil values or preparing content previews.

Phoenix automatically associates the `BookController` with the `BookView` unless you specify a different one.

End-to-End Flow

Let's walk through how everything connects using your browser request to `/books`.

Router matches `GET /books` to `BookController.index`.

Controller prepares data (e.g., `books = Library.list_books()`).

Render call sends the data to the view and selects the template.

View may contain helpers to format the data.

Template receives the data and produces HTML for the browser.

This flow keeps each part of the application focused on a single responsibility:

The controller deals with *what to do*.

The view defines *how to prepare data for presentation.*

The template controls *how to display it to the user.*

Real-World Example: Listing Users

Suppose you want to show a list of users from the database. Start with your router:

```
get "/users", UserController, :index
```

Then your controller:

```
defmodule MyAppWeb.UserController do
  use MyAppWeb, :controller

  alias MyApp.Accounts

  def index(conn, _params) do
    users = Accounts.list_users()
    render(conn, :index, users: users)
  end
end
```

The context module:

```
defmodule MyApp.Accounts do
  alias MyApp.Repo
  alias MyApp.Accounts.User

  def list_users do
    Repo.all(User)
  end
end
```

And the template:

```
<!-- lib/my_app_web/templates/user/index.html.heex
-->
<h2>Registered Users</h2>
<ul>
<%= for user <- @users do %>
  <li><%= user.name %> - <%= user.email %></li>
<% end %>
```

```
</ul>
```

With just a few lines of code, you've now connected your router, controller, data layer, view helpers (if any), and template rendering into a full feature.

Controllers, views, and templates form the backbone of Phoenix's response cycle. Each one plays a distinct role:

Controllers are the decision-makers.

Views are the presenters.

Templates are the UI.

When you organize your application this way, it becomes easier to manage complexity, test behavior in isolation, and reuse formatting logic across different templates.

As you build more complex pages, you'll learn how to share view helpers, customize layouts, and even use components in HEEx to encapsulate reusable UI blocks.

Phoenix Contexts and Domain Logic

One of the design decisions that sets Phoenix apart from many other web frameworks is its emphasis on **contexts**. Contexts are modules that encapsulate and organize your domain logic—everything that defines the rules, behavior, and workflows of your application. Rather than scattering your business logic across controllers, schemas, and helpers, Phoenix encourages you to centralize it within clearly defined boundaries.

The goal of contexts is not just to structure your code but to create a clean **API layer** for each area of your application. This separation ensures that your web interface remains thin, and that your business logic is isolated, reusable, and easier to test.

In traditional MVC (Model-View-Controller) architectures, it's common to see database logic and business rules creeping into controllers or models. Over time, this leads to tangled code and poor separation of concerns.

Phoenix discourages this by introducing a middle layer: the context. You don't fetch records or perform operations directly inside controllers. Instead, you

69

delegate that responsibility to a context module. This design keeps controllers focused on the request/response cycle and ensures that domain rules are decoupled from your web interface.

Each context should represent a functional area of your application: things like `Accounts`, `Blog`, `Billing`, `Inventory`, or `Library`. Inside the context, you define functions like `create_user`, `list_books`, `register_account`, and so on. The web interface simply calls these functions—it doesn't know how they work internally.

Creating a Context: A Practical Walkthrough

Let's say you want to build a feature for managing books. Phoenix gives you a generator that scaffolds the context, schema, migration, and basic CRUD functions in one step:

```
mix phx.gen.context Library Book books title:string
author:string
```

This command generates multiple files:

A context module: `lib/my_app/library.ex`

A schema module: `lib/my_app/library/book.ex`

A database migration: `priv/repo/migrations/*_create_books.exs`

The context module will look like this:

```
defmodule MyApp.Library do
  @moduledoc """
  The Library context.
  """

  import Ecto.Query, warn: false
  alias MyApp.Repo
  alias MyApp.Library.Book

  def list_books do
    Repo.all(Book)
  end

  def get_book!(id), do: Repo.get!(Book, id)
```

```elixir
  def create_book(attrs \\ %{}) do
    %Book{}
    |> Book.changeset(attrs)
    |> Repo.insert()
  end

  def update_book(%Book{} = book, attrs) do
    book
    |> Book.changeset(attrs)
    |> Repo.update()
  end

  def delete_book(%Book{} = book) do
    Repo.delete(book)
  end

  def change_book(%Book{} = book, attrs \\ %{}) do
    Book.changeset(book, attrs)
  end
end
```

This module provides a clean API to manage books. You can now use it like so:

```elixir
MyApp.Library.list_books()
MyApp.Library.create_book(%{title: "Phoenix in
Action", author: "Geoff Harcourt"})
```

The corresponding schema lives in:

```
lib/my_app/library/book.ex
```

It looks like this:

```elixir
defmodule MyApp.Library.Book do
  use Ecto.Schema
  import Ecto.Changeset

  schema "books" do
    field :title, :string
    field :author, :string
```

```
      timestamps()
    end

    def changeset(book, attrs) do
      book
      |> cast(attrs, [:title, :author])
      |> validate_required([:title, :author])
    end
end
```

The `changeset/2` function is responsible for validating and transforming incoming data. This is where you enforce required fields, check types, and add custom validation rules. The controller never calls `Repo` directly—it always goes through the context, which calls the schema.

Before you can use the new schema, you need to apply the migration:

```
mix ecto.migrate
```

This creates the `books` table in your PostgreSQL database.

Using the Context in a Controller

In your controller, you should never call `Repo` or manually work with changesets. Always use your context functions:

```
defmodule MyAppWeb.BookController do
  use MyAppWeb, :controller

  alias MyApp.Library

  def index(conn, _params) do
    books = Library.list_books()
    render(conn, :index, books: books)
  end

  def show(conn, %{"id" => id}) do
    book = Library.get_book!(id)
    render(conn, :show, book: book)
  end
end
```

The controller only cares about routing and rendering—it delegates everything else to the context.

Writing Your Own Context Functions

The generator provides CRUD operations, but you can add more behavior as your application grows.

Suppose you want a function that lists all books by a specific author:

```
def list_books_by_author(author) do
  Book
  |> where([b], b.author == ^author)
  |> Repo.all()
end
```

You now have a single, reusable function that encapsulates the query. The rest of your app doesn't need to know how it works internally.

You can also add more complex logic here, like custom filters, analytics, or business rules that apply when certain actions are taken.

Testing Contexts in Isolation

Contexts are very easy to test because they don't depend on controllers or views. You can write unit tests that only verify the behavior of the context and the data it returns.

Here's a simple test:

```
test "list_books_by_author/1 returns only matching
books" do
  Library.create_book(%{title: "One", author:
"Ada"})
  Library.create_book(%{title: "Two", author:
"Bob"})

  results = Library.list_books_by_author("Ada")
  assert length(results) == 1
  assert Enum.any?(results, &(&1.author == "Ada"))
end
```

Because contexts isolate your domain logic, you can write fast, focused tests that catch problems early.

73

Best Practices When Designing Contexts

Name them around a domain concept, not a database table. Use `Accounts`, not `Users`.

Don't overstuff one context. Split functionality if your module starts doing too much.

Expose only what's needed. Avoid leaking internal schema details from your context's public functions.

Use contexts in controllers, not schemas. Controllers shouldn't call `Repo` or changesets directly.

Group related functionality. Don't create a context just to match a single schema; create it to reflect a cohesive domain boundary.

Phoenix contexts are how you structure domain logic around real application boundaries. They form a public API for your features. Inside the context, you manage how to query, create, update, and delete data. You also encode your rules, validations, and workflows there.

By using contexts correctly, your application becomes more modular, maintainable, and testable. Each part of your app—controllers, templates, live views—can interact with the domain in a consistent way, without needing to know internal details.

Database Integration with Ecto

Ecto is the primary database library used in Elixir and Phoenix. It's not just an ORM. It provides a full suite of tools for defining schemas, writing queries, performing validations, and managing database migrations—all while staying true to functional programming principles.

In Phoenix, Ecto is integrated tightly from the start. When you generate a new Phoenix project, Ecto is already configured for you. The default database is PostgreSQL, but Ecto also supports MySQL, SQLite, and other adapters via community-maintained libraries.

Schema: Mapping Elixir to Your Database

At the core of Ecto is the **schema**—a module that maps a table in your database to a struct in your application. Schemas are defined using `Ecto.Schema`.

Here's an example:

```
defmodule MyApp.Library.Book do
  use Ecto.Schema
  import Ecto.Changeset

  schema "books" do
    field :title, :string
    field :author, :string
    field :published_at, :date

    timestamps()
  end
end
```

This defines a struct `%Book{}` that maps to a `books` table. Fields like `:title`, `:author`, and `:published_at` represent columns in the table. The `timestamps()` macro automatically adds `inserted_at` and `updated_at` fields.

Once you define a schema, you can use it to build queries, changesets, and perform inserts or updates via Ecto.

Migrations: Structuring and Evolving Your Database

Migrations are versioned scripts that modify your database schema—adding tables, fields, indexes, constraints, and more. You can generate a migration with:

```
mix ecto.gen.migration add_books_table
```

This creates a file under `priv/repo/migrations/`. Open the file and define your table:

```
defmodule MyApp.Repo.Migrations.AddBooksTable do
  use Ecto.Migration

  def change do
    create table(:books) do
      add :title, :string, null: false
```

```
        add :author, :string, null: false
        add :published_at, :date

        timestamps()
      end
  end
end
```

Apply the migration with:

```
mix ecto.migrate
```

Your `books` table is now live in the database, ready to be used by your schema.

If you need to roll it back:

```
mix ecto.rollback
```

Ecto's migrations are reversible by default when you use the `change` function, which supports automatic rollback. For more complex operations, you can define `up` and `down` functions manually.

Queries: Reading Data with Ecto.Query

Ecto provides a composable and expressive query syntax through the `Ecto.Query` module.

You can write queries like this:

```
import Ecto.Query

query = from b in Book,
        where: b.author == "Ada Lovelace",
        order_by: [asc: b.title]

Repo.all(query)
```

Or using the pipe operator:

```
Book

|> where([b], b.author == "Ada Lovelace")

|> order_by([b], asc: b.title)
```

```
|> Repo.all()
```

Both examples fetch books by a specific author and order them by title. The pipe style is often easier to read and better suited for chaining conditions incrementally.

You can also fetch a single record:

```
Repo.get(Book, 1)                # by ID

Repo.get_by(Book, title: "Elixir in Action")
```

Ecto returns `nil` if the record isn't found, or raises with `Repo.get!/2` and `Repo.get_by!/2`.

Inserts, Updates, and Deletes: Using Changesets

To create or modify records, Ecto requires you to build a **changeset**. A changeset is a data structure that wraps your data with validations and transformation logic.

Here's a changeset function:

```
def changeset(book, attrs) do
  book
  |> cast(attrs, [:title, :author, :published_at])
  |> validate_required([:title, :author])
  |> validate_length(:title, min: 3)
end
```

This function:

Accepts a struct (usually `%Book{}`) and a map of attributes.

Casts only the allowed fields.

Validates presence and string length.

To insert a new book:

```
attrs = %{

  title: "Programming Phoenix",
```

77

```
  author: "Chris McCord",

  published_at: ~D[2020-04-01]

}


%Book{}

|> Book.changeset(attrs)

|> Repo.insert()
```

To update an existing book:

```
book = Repo.get!(Book, 1)

book
|> Book.changeset(%{title: "Updated Title"})
|> Repo.update()
```

To delete:

```
Repo.delete(book)
```

You can also preview the changes without saving by using the `change/2` function or `Ecto.Changeset.apply_changes/1`.

Filtering and Joining Data

Ecto lets you write complex queries with joins and filters while keeping your code composable and readable.

For example, if you had an `Author` schema and a book belongs to an author:

```
defmodule MyApp.Library.Author do
  use Ecto.Schema

  schema "authors" do
    field :name, :string
    has_many :books, MyApp.Library.Book
  end
end
```

```
defmodule MyApp.Library.Book do
  use Ecto.Schema

  schema "books" do
    field :title, :string
    belongs_to :author, MyApp.Library.Author

    timestamps()
  end
end
```

Then you could fetch all books with their authors like this:

```
Book
```

```
|> join(:inner, [b], a in assoc(b, :author))
|> preload([b, a], author: a)
|> Repo.all()
```

This efficiently joins and preloads associated data without N+1 query problems.

Ecto.Multi: Handling Transactions

Sometimes, you need to perform multiple database operations atomically. Ecto provides `Ecto.Multi` to help you do this declaratively.

Here's how to insert an author and book together in a single transaction:

```
Ecto.Multi.new()

|> Ecto.Multi.insert(:author, %Author{name: "Jane
Austen"})

|> Ecto.Multi.insert(:book, fn %{author: author} ->

    %Book{title: "Emma", author_id: author.id}

    |> Book.changeset(%{})

  end)

|> Repo.transaction()
```

This ensures both inserts succeed or both fail together.

Working with Dates and UUIDs

PostgreSQL has excellent support for date/time types, and Ecto maps those into Elixir `Date`, `Time`, and `NaiveDateTime` types. Use `~D[YYYY-MM-DD]` for dates and `~N[YYYY-MM-DD HH:MM:SS]` for naive datetimes.

If you want to use UUIDs instead of integers for primary keys, you can configure your migration and schema like so:

```
create table(:users, primary_key: false) do
  add :id, :binary_id, primary_key: true
  add :email, :string
end
```

And in your schema:

```
@primary_key {:id, :binary_id, autogenerate: true}
@derive {Phoenix.Param, key: :id}
schema "users" do
  field :email, :string
end
```

This gives you cleaner URLs and more secure identifiers.

Ecto gives you a complete toolkit for database interaction—without hiding SQL, and without sacrificing safety or expressiveness. You work directly with Elixir structs, using transformations and pattern matching, while writing readable queries and safely validating user input.

Every part of your Phoenix application—contexts, controllers, LiveViews—can depend on Ecto to perform consistent, testable, and reliable operations.

Chapter 5: Real-Time User Interfaces with Phoenix LiveView

Modern users expect web interfaces to be fast, responsive, and reactive. They want real-time feedback when filling out forms, instant updates when data changes, and fluid interactions without reloading the page. Traditionally, this meant writing JavaScript-heavy frontends with client-side frameworks like React or Vue, and then integrating them with your backend through APIs.

Phoenix LiveView changes that model entirely.

LiveView allows you to build rich, real-time web interfaces using only Elixir and HEEx templates—no custom JavaScript required for most interactions. It opens the door to dynamic, interactive features while preserving server-side rendering and application state.

Understanding LiveView

Phoenix LiveView is one of the most important innovations in web development today because it allows you to build interactive, real-time web applications without writing complex JavaScript. Everything happens on the server using Elixir, yet the user experience remains fast, smooth, and highly responsive. To really grasp the power of LiveView, you need to understand how it works under the hood and how it changes the way applications are traditionally built.

At its core, LiveView works by setting up a **persistent WebSocket connection** between the client (the browser) and the server (your Phoenix backend). Initially, the page is rendered just like any normal Phoenix page: the server renders the HTML and sends it to the client. But once the page loads, instead of relying on JavaScript to handle user interactions like button clicks or form changes, LiveView intercepts those events and sends them back to the server over the WebSocket. Your LiveView module then processes the event, updates the state, and re-renders only the part of the page that changed.

Because the server always holds the source of truth, your application logic, validation, and real-time behavior all happen in one place. There's no need to maintain two separate codebases—one in the backend (Elixir) and another in the frontend (JavaScript).

Building a Simple LiveView: Step-by-Step

Suppose you want to build a simple counter that increases or decreases every time a button is clicked.

First, create a LiveView module:

```elixir
defmodule MyAppWeb.CounterLive do
  use Phoenix.LiveView

  def mount(_params, _session, socket) do
    {:ok, assign(socket, count: 0)}
  end

  def render(assigns) do
    ~H"""
    <div class="counter">
      <h1>Counter: <%= @count %></h1>
      <button phx-click="increment">+</button>
      <button phx-click="decrement">-</button>
    </div>
    """
  end

  def handle_event("increment", _params, socket) do
    {:noreply, update(socket, :count, &(&1 + 1))}
  end

  def handle_event("decrement", _params, socket) do
    {:noreply, update(socket, :count, &(&1 - 1))}
  end
end
```

Here's what each part does:

mount/3 is called when the LiveView is first mounted. It initializes the socket's state, in this case setting count to 0.

render/1 defines the HTML that gets shown to the user. Notice the phx-click="increment" and phx-click="decrement" attributes on the buttons. These tell Phoenix to send an event back to the server when clicked.

`handle_event/3` responds to the events. It updates the state of the socket (the `count`) and triggers a re-render with the new value.

To wire this up, add a route to your router:

```
# lib/my_app_web/router.ex
scope "/", MyAppWeb do
  pipe_through :browser

  live "/counter", CounterLive
end
```

Now, when you visit `http://localhost:4000/counter`, you see the counter page. Clicking the buttons updates the number immediately—no page reloads, no heavy frontend libraries.

The Lifecycle of a LiveView

Understanding LiveView also means understanding its lifecycle, which runs through distinct stages:

Static HTML Render (Initial Request): When a user first visits a LiveView page, Phoenix renders a fully static HTML page just like a regular controller would. This ensures SEO friendliness and fast initial page load.

WebSocket Connection Establishment: After the static HTML is loaded, the browser initiates a WebSocket connection to the server. This connection is lightweight and allows bidirectional communication.

Mounting the LiveView: Once the WebSocket is established, the `mount/3` function is called again (over the socket this time). This allows you to perform setup that depends on real-time session data or authenticated user info.

Stateful Interactivity: From this point onward, every user action—clicks, form submissions, etc.—triggers server-side `handle_event/3` callbacks. After processing, the server sends tiny diffs (only what changed) back to the client.

Efficient DOM Patching: The client-side JavaScript (Phoenix's `phoenix_live_view.js`) applies these diffs efficiently using a library called `morphdom`. It updates only the parts of the DOM that changed.

83

This entire process gives your users the experience of a "single-page application" without writing a traditional client-heavy application.

Handling User Input

LiveView can handle form inputs, validations, and dynamic user interfaces in real time.

Here's an example of a LiveView that validates a username field as the user types:

```
defmodule MyAppWeb.UsernameLive do
  use Phoenix.LiveView

  def mount(_params, _session, socket) do
    {:ok, assign(socket, username: "", valid:
true)}
  end

  def render(assigns) do
    ~H"""
    <form phx-change="validate">
      <input name="username" value={@username}
placeholder="Choose a username"/>
      <%= if @valid do %>
        <span style="color:
green;">Available</span>
      <% else %>
        <span style="color: red;">Taken</span>
      <% end %>
    </form>
    """
  end

  def handle_event("validate", %{"username" =>
username}, socket) do
    valid = username_available?(username)
    {:noreply, assign(socket, username: username,
valid: valid)}
  end

  defp username_available?(username) do
    username not in ["admin", "test", "user"]
```

```
    end
end
```

Every time the input changes, the `validate` event is triggered, which checks if the username is available. The feedback is immediate, giving a seamless experience.

Optimizing LiveView Performance

Because LiveView operates over a WebSocket, efficiency matters. Here are some techniques you can use:

Limit Assigns: Only assign necessary data. Avoid assigning large datasets unless absolutely required.

Use Temporary Assigns: If you have data that you only need for one render and then can drop, use `temporary_assigns`:

```
assign(socket, temporary_assigns: [flash: nil])
```

Minimize Event Volume: Avoid firing events unnecessarily. Use debounce/throttle options for inputs if necessary:

```
<input phx-debounce="500" name="search" placeholder="Type to
search..."/>
```

This limits the number of events sent to the server when a user types.

When to Use LiveView

LiveView is particularly well-suited for:

Interactive forms with live validation

Real-time dashboards

Chat interfaces

Live search and filtering

Multiplayer games or collaborative apps

Admin panels with dynamic updates

Notifications and activity feeds

In all these cases, LiveView removes the complexity of building a separate frontend stack and instead lets you work fully in Elixir, keeping your application simpler and your system more maintainable.

LiveView brings a new model to web development. Instead of splitting your application into a backend and a separate frontend, you keep your logic unified, powerful, and server-driven. You get full real-time interactivity, easy debugging, strong type-safety, and the scalability benefits of running on the BEAM—all without needing to build a JavaScript-heavy frontend.

With LiveView, you can focus on what matters: building features and delivering great user experiences.

Building Live Components

As your Phoenix LiveView applications grow, managing everything inside a single LiveView module can quickly become messy. Handling multiple parts of a complex page—different forms, dynamic lists, sections that update independently—calls for a better organizational strategy. That's where **Live Components** come in.

Live Components allow you to split your LiveView interfaces into smaller, reusable, isolated pieces. They encapsulate behavior and state, making your LiveView apps easier to scale, easier to maintain, and easier to reason about. You can think of a Live Component as a mini LiveView that lives inside a parent LiveView but doesn't require a separate process unless you want it to.

There are two types of components you'll work with:

Function components – stateless, very lightweight, pure rendering components.

Stateful Live Components – components that manage their own local state and handle events.

Building Function Components

Function components are simple and stateless. They take assigns (data passed from the parent), render HTML, and nothing more. They're perfect for small, reusable pieces of UI like badges, buttons, cards, or table rows.

You define a function component using `Phoenix.Component`:

```
defmodule MyAppWeb.UIComponents do
  use Phoenix.Component

  def badge(assigns) do
    ~H"""
    <span class="badge"><%= @label %></span>
    """
  end
end
```

This `badge/1` function receives an `assigns` map and renders a badge. You can use this component in your LiveView or template like this:

```
<.badge label="New!" />
```

Notice the syntax `<.badge />`. That's Phoenix's HEEx component syntax. It feels very close to HTML and keeps your templates clean.

Function components:

Have no internal state.

Are very fast to render.

Cannot handle events directly.

If you only need rendering, function components should be your first choice.

Building Stateful Live Components

Stateful Live Components are more powerful. They manage their own local state, can handle events, and allow you to create isolated, interactive pieces inside a LiveView without the overhead of full processes unless you explicitly set it up.

You define a Live Component by using `Phoenix.LiveComponent`:

```
defmodule MyAppWeb.TodoItemComponent do
  use Phoenix.LiveComponent

  def render(assigns) do
    ~H"""
    <div id={"todo-#{@id}"} class={"todo-item #{if
@done, do: "done"}"}>
```

87

```
      <input type="checkbox" phx-click="toggle"
phx-target={@myself} <%= if @done, do: "checked" %>
/>
      <span><%= @title %></span>
    </div>
    """
  end

  def handle_event("toggle", _params, socket) do
    {:noreply, assign(socket, :done,
!socket.assigns.done)}
  end
end
```

Here's what happens in this component:

It renders a checkbox for a todo item.

It responds to a click event on the checkbox (phx-click="toggle").

It uses @myself as the phx-target, meaning the event is scoped to this component, not the parent LiveView.

It updates its local state (:done) when toggled.

To use a Live Component inside a LiveView:

```
<.live_component

  module={MyAppWeb.TodoItemComponent}

  id={todo.id}

  title={todo.title}

  done={todo.done}

/>
```

You must always provide a unique id to each Live Component. Phoenix uses the id to track and patch components efficiently.

Notice that the assigns passed when mounting the component (title, done, etc.) are merged into the component's local socket state.

Managing Component Events

When a Live Component fires an event (like `toggle` in the example above), the event is handled inside the component itself if `phx-target` points to `@myself`. Otherwise, it bubbles up to the parent LiveView if no target is specified.

This gives you very fine-grained control:

Local events stay inside the component.

Higher-level events can be delegated to the parent when necessary.

If you want a component to notify the parent LiveView about changes (like broadcasting an update), you can use `send/2`:

```
send(self(), {:todo_updated, %{id: @id, done: @done}})
```

Then the parent LiveView can handle it with `handle_info/2`.

This pattern is useful when you want to build components that affect global state, like a shopping cart item component sending a message when its quantity changes.

Live Components vs Full LiveViews

Live Components are embedded inside a parent LiveView process. They don't have independent processes of their own. This makes them lightweight and efficient.

However, if you need a component that has its own connection, lifecycle, or should survive the parent crashing, you would create a **nested LiveView** instead of a Live Component.

You embed a full nested LiveView like this:

```
live_render(socket, MyAppWeb.ChatLive, id: :chat)
```

For most use cases inside a page—form fields, lists, tabs, etc.—Live Components are what you want. Only reach for nested LiveViews when you truly need independent processes.

Real-World Example: A Voting Widget

Let's build a small voting widget where users can upvote or downvote posts.

Here's the Live Component:

```elixir
defmodule MyAppWeb.VoteComponent do
  use Phoenix.LiveComponent

  def render(assigns) do
    ~H"""
    <div id={"vote-#{@id}"}>
      <h3><%= @title %></h3>
      <p>Votes: <%= @votes %></p>
      <button phx-click="upvote" phx-
target={@myself}>+</button>
      <button phx-click="downvote" phx-
target={@myself}>-</button>
    </div>
    """
  end

  def handle_event("upvote", _params, socket) do
    {:noreply, update(socket, :votes, &(&1 + 1))}
  end

  def handle_event("downvote", _params, socket) do
    {:noreply, update(socket, :votes, &(&1 - 1))}
  end
end
```

And usage inside your LiveView:

```elixir
<%= for post <- @posts do %>
  <.live_component
    module={MyAppWeb.VoteComponent}
    id={post.id}
    title={post.title}
    votes={post.votes}
  />
<% end %>
```

Each voting widget works independently without interfering with the others. All behavior is cleanly encapsulated.

Benefits of Using Live Components

Isolation: Each component manages its own rendering and local state.

Reusability: Components can be reused across different LiveViews or templates.

Clarity: Smaller, focused components make it easier to understand and reason about your interface.

Efficiency: LiveView automatically tracks and diffs components separately for minimal updates.

As your application grows, Live Components help you keep complexity under control, ensuring that each piece of your interface stays maintainable and testable.

LiveView Lifecycle and Performance Optimization

To build high-performance real-time interfaces with Phoenix LiveView, it's essential to understand the lifecycle of a LiveView process. Every LiveView goes through a series of well-defined phases, from initial rendering to socket connection, state updates, and DOM patching. Mastering this lifecycle enables you to optimize performance, manage data efficiently, and handle user interactions with precision.

The Lifecycle: From Mount to Patch

When a client requests a LiveView route (e.g., `/dashboard`), the server renders a static HTML version of the view. This initial rendering is just a regular controller-style HTML response and is fully crawlable and indexable.

As soon as the page loads in the browser, a JavaScript client bundled with Phoenix (`phoenix_live_view.js`) establishes a WebSocket connection back to the server. This is where the real-time magic begins.

Here's a breakdown of what happens behind the scenes:

Initial Render (static HTML)

The `render/1` function is called during the initial HTTP request.

LiveView renders a full HTML layout server-side.

WebSocket Connection is established

The browser connects via WebSocket.

LiveView resumes execution in a persistent process.

Mounting the LiveView (mount/3)

Called again, now over the socket.

Here you fetch data, assign state, subscribe to topics, or start background tasks.

State Assignment and Updates

All updates go through `assign/2` or `assign/3`.

LiveView tracks what data changes and automatically re-renders the necessary parts.

DOM Patch and Re-rendering

LiveView compares the previous rendered view with the new one using a virtual DOM.

It sends the minimal diff to the browser.

The client applies those changes using DOM patching.

This cycle repeats as long as the user interacts with the LiveView. You stay on the same page, over the same connection, while the server keeps pushing stateful updates.

Understanding mount/3

The `mount/3` function is where your LiveView initializes. It's the first thing you write in every LiveView module. Here's a typical example:

```
def mount(_params, _session, socket) do
  if connected?(socket) do
    MyApp.PubSub.subscribe("notifications")
  end

  {:ok, assign(socket, count: 0, notifications:
[])}
end
```

Use `connected?/1` to determine if you're in the WebSocket phase.

Use it to conditionally start background work, subscribe to topics, or fetch live data.

Avoid expensive operations during the static render phase (when `connected?/1` is false).

If you try to query the database or subscribe to PubSub before the socket is connected, you'll introduce performance issues or errors. The mount function gives you full control to delay real-time behavior until the connection is ready.

Handling Events Efficiently

LiveView processes events using the `handle_event/3` callback:

```elixir
def handle_event("increment", _params, socket) do

  {:noreply, update(socket, :count, &(&1 + 1))}

end
```

Each user interaction—clicks, inputs, key presses—can be wired to `phx-click`, `phx-submit`, or `phx-change`. These attributes send the event to the server where `handle_event/3` processes it.
To optimize event handling:

Keep the state small. Only assign what you need to render.

Debounce or throttle noisy events (like key presses):

```html
<input type="text" phx-debounce="300" name="query" />
```
This delays sending events until the user pauses typing, reducing network traffic and CPU usage.

Temporary Assigns for Short-Lived State

By default, all assigns in LiveView persist across renders. But sometimes, you want a value to exist for only one render—for example, a flash message or a transient result.

LiveView provides `temporary_assigns` for this:

```
def mount(_params, _session, socket) do
  socket =
    socket
    |> assign(:notification, nil)
    |> assign(temporary_assigns: [notification:
nil])

  {:ok, socket}
end
```

This ensures :notification is cleared after each render. It improves memory usage and keeps your socket state small.

Another use case: rendering large datasets that are fetched once but not retained in memory.

```
assign(socket, items: fetch_items(),
temporary_assigns: [items: []])
```

Using handle_info/2 for Background Work

In addition to user-triggered events, you can handle background messages with handle_info/2. This is useful for polling, scheduled tasks, or PubSub events.

```
def mount(_params, _session, socket) do
  if connected?(socket), do:
Process.send_after(self(), :tick, 1000)
  {:ok, assign(socket, time: DateTime.utc_now())}
end

def handle_info(:tick, socket) do
  Process.send_after(self(), :tick, 1000)
  {:noreply, assign(socket, time:
DateTime.utc_now())}
end
```

This sets up a recurring clock that updates the UI every second. Since LiveView maintains the WebSocket connection, this all happens without client-side timers or polling libraries.

You can also handle PubSub messages:

```
def handle_info(%{event: "new_message", payload:
message}, socket) do
  {:noreply, update(socket, :messages, fn msgs ->
[message | msgs] end)}
end
```

This makes LiveView ideal for real-time features like chat, alerts, feeds, or dashboards.

Reducing Latency and Payload Size

A few techniques to boost LiveView performance:

Avoid over-assigning. Don't assign data unless it's used in the template.

Use streaming for large lists with `Phoenix.LiveView.stream/3`.

Preload associations before rendering to avoid N+1 queries.

Avoid re-rendering static sections by extracting them into `function components`.

Example:

```
defmodule MyAppWeb.Components.UserCard do
  use Phoenix.Component

  def user_card(assigns) do
    ~H"""
    <div class="card">
      <h2><%= @user.name %></h2>
      <p><%= @user.email %></p>
    </div>
    """
  end
end
```
Use it like:

```
<.user_card user={user} />
```

This way, Phoenix can patch and isolate changes more efficiently.

Process Lifecycle and Cleanup

Each LiveView is backed by a process. When the user navigates away or closes the tab, that process is terminated. You can hook into that event using the `terminate/2` callback:

```
def terminate(_reason, socket) do
  Logger.info("LiveView terminated:
#{inspect(socket.assigns)}")
  :ok
end
```

Use this for cleanup, analytics, or logging.

The lifecycle of a Phoenix LiveView—from mount to teardown—is predictable, composable, and optimized for interactive real-time behavior. Performance tuning starts with understanding how state is managed, when updates happen, and how much data gets assigned and rendered. With techniques like temporary assigns, throttled events, streaming, and isolated components, you can build real-time web interfaces that are not only rich in functionality but also exceptionally fast and efficient.

Practical Real-Time Applications

Now that you understand how LiveView works, how to manage its lifecycle, and how to optimize its performance, it's time to apply that knowledge to building actual real-time applications. This is where LiveView truly shines— bridging the gap between traditional server-rendered applications and modern interactive user experiences. In this section, you'll build fully interactive features that respond to user actions, external data, and other users—all without relying on custom JavaScript.

Each example will be written in clear, functional Elixir, using HEEx templates and LiveView events. You'll learn how to structure real-time behavior, maintain consistent state, and deliver high responsiveness even under concurrent use.

Live Search with Instant Feedback

Let's start with a common feature: real-time search.

This is the interface:

As the user types into the input field, the backend searches the database and returns matching results.

Feedback is instant, no page reload, no form submission.

LiveView Module:

```elixir
defmodule MyAppWeb.BookSearchLive do
  use Phoenix.LiveView
  alias MyApp.Library

  def mount(_params, _session, socket) do
    {:ok, assign(socket, query: "", results: [])}
  end

  def render(assigns) do
    ~H"""
    <div>
      <input type="text" name="query"
value={@query} placeholder="Search books..."
              phx-change="search" phx-
debounce="300"/>

      <ul>
      <%= for book <- @results do %>
        <li><%= book.title %> by <%= book.author
%></li>
      <% end %>
      </ul>
    </div>
    """
  end

  def handle_event("search", %{"query" => query},
socket) do
    results = if String.trim(query) != "", do:
Library.search_books(query), else: []
    {:noreply, assign(socket, query: query,
results: results)}
  end
end
```

Context Function:

```
def search_books(query) do
  from(b in Book, where: ilike(b.title,
^"%#{query}%"))
  |> Repo.all()
end
```

You now have a working, real-time search input. It reacts after 300ms of inactivity to reduce load, and results update dynamically as the user types.

Live Form Validation

Forms are at the heart of most applications. With LiveView, you can validate them as users type—without waiting for form submission or introducing JavaScript.

LiveView for Real-Time Validation:

```
defmodule MyAppWeb.RegistrationLive do
  use Phoenix.LiveView
  alias MyApp.Accounts
  alias MyApp.Accounts.User

  def mount(_params, _session, socket) do
    changeset = Accounts.change_user(%User{})
    {:ok, assign(socket, changeset: changeset)}
  end

  def render(assigns) do
    ~H"""
    <.form let={f} for={@changeset} phx-
change="validate" phx-submit="save">
      <%= label f, :email %>
      <%= text_input f, :email %>
      <%= error_tag f, :email %>

      <%= label f, :password %>
      <%= password_input f, :password %>
      <%= error_tag f, :password %>

      <button type="submit">Register</button>
    </.form>
    """
  end
```

```elixir
  def handle_event("validate", %{"user" =>
user_params}, socket) do
    changeset =
      %User{}
      |> Accounts.change_user(user_params)
      |> Map.put(:action, :validate)

    {:noreply, assign(socket, changeset:
changeset)}
  end

  def handle_event("save", %{"user" =>
user_params}, socket) do
    case Accounts.register_user(user_params) do
      {:ok, _user} ->
        {:noreply, push_redirect(socket, to:
"/welcome")}
      {:error, changeset} ->
        {:noreply, assign(socket, changeset:
changeset)}
    end
  end
end
```

As the user types, errors appear in real time. This reduces friction and improves usability significantly.

Real-Time Chat with PubSub

LiveView integrates seamlessly with Phoenix PubSub to support real-time messaging between users.

LiveView Module:

```elixir
defmodule MyAppWeb.ChatLive do
  use Phoenix.LiveView
  alias MyAppWeb.Endpoint

  def mount(_params, _session, socket) do
    if connected?(socket), do:
Endpoint.subscribe("chat:lobby")
```

```elixir
    {:ok, assign(socket, message: "", messages:
[])}
  end

  def render(assigns) do
    ~H"""
    <div>
      <div id="chat-box">
        <%= for msg <- @messages do %>
          <p><%= msg %></p>
        <% end %>
      </div>

      <form phx-submit="send">
        <input name="message" value={@message} phx-
change="update"/>
        <button type="submit">Send</button>
      </form>
    </div>
    """
  end

  def handle_event("update", %{"message" => msg},
socket) do
    {:noreply, assign(socket, message: msg)}
  end

  def handle_event("send", %{"message" => msg},
socket) do
    Endpoint.broadcast("chat:lobby", "new_message",
msg)
    {:noreply, assign(socket, message: "")}
  end

  def handle_info(%{event: "new_message", payload:
msg}, socket) do
    {:noreply, update(socket, :messages, fn msgs ->
msgs ++ [msg] end)}
  end
end
```

Every connected client subscribed to `"chat:lobby"` receives the new message and updates their UI. There's no polling, no manual refresh—just clean, efficient real-time messaging.

Live Dashboard Updates

You can build live dashboards that reflect backend events like new orders, user logins, or server metrics using background updates and PubSub.

Here's a simplified counter that updates every 2 seconds:

```
defmodule MyAppWeb.MetricsLive do
  use Phoenix.LiveView

  def mount(_params, _session, socket) do
    if connected?(socket), do: schedule_tick()
    {:ok, assign(socket, metric: get_metric())}
  end

  def handle_info(:tick, socket) do
    schedule_tick()
    {:noreply, assign(socket, metric:
get_metric())}
  end

  defp schedule_tick do
    Process.send_after(self(), :tick, 2_000)
  end

  defp get_metric do
    :rand.uniform(100)
  end

  def render(assigns) do
    ~H"""
    <div>
      <h2>Current metric: <%= @metric %></h2>
    </div>
    """
  end
end
```

In a production system, `get_metric/0` would fetch live stats from Redis, the database, telemetry, or any monitoring system.

Presence-Based Features

You can track who is online, who's typing, or who's viewing a page with Phoenix Presence.

```
MyAppWeb.Presence.track(self(), "users:online",
user_id, %{name: user.name})
```

To fetch all online users:

```
MyAppWeb.Presence.list("users:online")
```

You can broadcast these changes and update the LiveView using `handle_info/2`, just like chat messages. It enables features like live typing indicators, online user lists, and collaborative editing indicators.

LiveView gives you a unified, server-side approach to building real-time web applications. Whether you're building live search, reactive forms, dashboards, messaging systems, or collaborative tools, LiveView handles everything with Elixir, over WebSockets, in a highly scalable and maintainable way.

Instead of gluing together frontend frameworks and APIs, you build entire features in one language, one process, and one mental model—keeping everything real-time, reactive, and reliable.

Chapter 6: Mastering Channels and WebSockets

LiveView makes it easy to build real-time user interfaces, but underneath it all, Phoenix's foundational technology for real-time communication is its channel system. Channels are what power LiveView, and they're also what you reach for when you need full control over WebSocket-based systems—especially in cases where LiveView isn't a good fit, such as mobile apps, custom frontend frameworks, or multiplayer games.

This chapter takes you deeper into the **anatomy of Phoenix channels**, how **PubSub powers distributed messaging**, how to **track state using Phoenix Presence**, and how to **scale channel-based applications** across nodes and data centers. If you're building real-time features beyond the browser—mobile sync, game sessions, collaborative editing, IoT messaging—Phoenix Channels are the tool you want.

Anatomy of Phoenix Channels

Phoenix Channels are designed to make real-time communication first-class in your web application. While HTTP is inherently stateless and unidirectional—each request starts and ends with the client—channels let you maintain an open, bidirectional connection between the client and server, built on top of WebSockets (with long-poll fallback if needed). Once established, this connection allows either side to push messages at any time.

In Phoenix, a channel is not just a connection pipe—it's a process. Each client that connects to a channel spawns its own isolated, supervised process in the BEAM. This makes channels incredibly robust and scalable out of the box. You're not managing connections manually—you're writing clean Elixir code to respond to well-defined events.

Defining a Channel Module

A channel is just a module that uses `Phoenix.Channel`. Inside it, you define how to authenticate clients, which topics they can join, and how to handle the events they push.

Here's a simple, working example for a chat room channel:

```elixir
defmodule MyAppWeb.ChatChannel do
  use Phoenix.Channel

  def join("chat:lobby", _payload, socket) do
    {:ok, socket}
  end

  def handle_in("new_message", %{"body" => body},
socket) do
    broadcast!(socket, "new_message", %{body:
body})
    {:noreply, socket}
  end
end
```

Let's break that down.

The `join/3` function determines whether a client is allowed to join a given topic. The first argument is the **topic string** (`"chat:lobby"`). The second is the payload sent by the client during the join. The third is the socket representing the client connection.

In this case, any client can join `"chat:lobby"` and immediately starts receiving messages. Once joined, the client can send messages via `push`, which will be handled by `handle_in/3`.

In `handle_in/3`, the server receives a `"new_message"` event, with a payload (a map containing `"body"`), and then broadcasts that message to all other clients on the same topic.

The broadcast happens via:

```elixir
broadcast!(socket, "new_message", %{body: body})
```

This pushes the message out to every other connected socket on the topic, including the sender.

You return `{:noreply, socket}` when you're not closing the connection or replying directly.

Connecting Clients: User Socket Setup

To use channels, you define a user socket module and tell Phoenix how to route incoming socket connections.

Create the socket module:

```
defmodule MyAppWeb.UserSocket do
  use Phoenix.Socket

  channel "chat:*", MyAppWeb.ChatChannel

  def connect(_params, socket, _connect_info) do
    {:ok, socket}
  end

  def id(_socket), do: nil
end
```

The `channel` macro maps any topic that matches `"chat:*"` to the `ChatChannel`. For example, `"chat:lobby"` or `"chat:room1"` would both match.

The `connect/3` function runs when a client tries to establish a WebSocket connection. This is where you can authenticate the user by checking params or tokens. You can also assign metadata to the socket.

The `id/1` function defines a unique identifier for this socket process. If you want to target this user later (e.g. force logout), you can use the `id` to broadcast a disconnect.

You plug this socket into the endpoint:

```
# in lib/my_app_web/endpoint.ex

socket "/socket", MyAppWeb.UserSocket,

  websocket: true,

  longpoll: false
```

This defines the WebSocket route at `/socket`.

Connecting from the Client (JavaScript)

Phoenix includes a JavaScript client library that handles connecting, joining, and pushing events.

First, include it in your app's frontend (Phoenix includes it by default):

```javascript
import {Socket} from "phoenix"

let socket = new Socket("/socket", {params:
{userToken: "123"}})
socket.connect()

let channel = socket.channel("chat:lobby", {})
channel.join()
  .receive("ok", resp => console.log("Joined
successfully", resp))
  .receive("error", resp => console.log("Unable to
join", resp))

channel.push("new_message", {body: "Hello from
client"})
```

You can now listen for incoming messages from the server:

```javascript
channel.on("new_message", payload => {
  console.log("New message received:",
payload.body)
})
```

This enables a fully interactive real-time experience. You've established a persistent WebSocket, subscribed to a topic, and wired up bidirectional communication—all with just a few lines on both ends.

Broadcasting and Handling Server Events

When you call broadcast!/3, Phoenix sends that event to every process subscribed to the topic. That includes the sender. If you don't want the sender to receive the event, use broadcast_from!/4 instead:

```elixir
broadcast_from!(socket, "new_message", %{body:
body})
```

This is useful in collaborative apps or chat rooms where you want the sender to update their state differently than everyone else.

You can also reply directly to a client:

```elixir
def handle_in("ping", _payload, socket) do
  {:reply, {:ok, %{response: "pong"}}, socket}
end
```

The client can then receive the reply using:

```javascript
channel.push("ping", {}).receive("ok", resp =>
console.log(resp))
```

Topic Namespacing and Design

Topics can be as granular as you like. A common pattern is to use scoped topics such as:

`"chat:room123"` – per chat room

`"document:42"` – per document in a collaborative editor

`"user:#{user_id}"` – for private notifications

`"orders:live"` – for real-time dashboards

Each topic becomes a logical channel instance. Phoenix automatically routes messages to the appropriate channel process for each client.

This gives you the flexibility to build highly personalized, multi-tenant, or partitioned systems while keeping all logic organized and secure.

Process Isolation and Fault Tolerance

Each joined channel is its own BEAM process. This is a huge architectural win. If a client misbehaves, crashes, or causes an error, only their own process is affected. The rest of the system keeps running.

For example, if you accidentally raise an exception in `handle_in/3`, Phoenix logs it and tears down only that connection.

You can supervise and monitor these processes using Elixir's tools. You can limit the number of connections, rate-limit events, or monitor crashes with `Telemetry`.

A Phoenix Channel is a persistent, concurrent process that serves as the entry point for real-time communication over WebSockets. Each client joins a topic, and from there, can push events, receive broadcasts, and participate in stateful, low-latency experiences—all with the power of Elixir's fault-tolerant runtime.

Topics, Events, and PubSub

Once you have a basic Phoenix Channel setup, the next step toward mastering real-time applications is understanding how **topics**, **events**, and **PubSub** work together. These three concepts are the building blocks that allow Phoenix to coordinate live communication, not just between clients and servers, but across different processes, applications, and even distributed clusters.

If you want to design real-time systems that are fast, scalable, and maintainable, it's important to get these foundations right. Let's unpack each one carefully, with practical examples you can apply immediately.

Topics: Structuring Communication Channels

In Phoenix, a **topic** is simply a string that groups clients together. When clients join a topic, they can send and receive messages tied to that topic.

A topic looks like this:

`"chat:lobby"`

It has two parts:

`"chat"` is the namespace (the category).

`"lobby"` is the specific instance (like a chat room ID or a resource ID).

You can structure topics however makes sense for your application. Here are real-world examples:

`"chat:room:42"` — A user in chat room 42.

`"document:12345"` — A collaborative editor session on document 12345.

`"user:17:notifications"` — Notifications channel for user ID 17.

When a client subscribes to a topic, it's only concerned with events on that specific topic. This lets you partition traffic cleanly and manage permissions easily.

Joining a topic is handled inside the channel's `join/3` function:

```elixir
def join("chat:lobby", _params, socket) do
  {:ok, socket}
end
```

You can even pattern-match on topic prefixes:

```elixir
def join("chat:" <> _room_id, _params, socket) do
  {:ok, socket}
end
```

This allows a single channel module to handle many dynamic topics.

Events: Sending and Receiving Actions

While the topic organizes *where* communication happens, an **event** describes *what* kind of action is happening within that topic.

An event is just a string label like:

```elixir
"new_message"
```

```elixir
"user_typing"
```

```elixir
"update_score"
```

```elixir
"file_uploaded"
```

Each event carries a **payload**—a map of data associated with the event.

In the channel, you handle incoming events using `handle_in/3`:

```elixir
def handle_in("new_message", %{"body" => body},
socket) do
  broadcast!(socket, "new_message", %{body: body})
  {:noreply, socket}
end
```

Here, when a user sends a `"new_message"` event, the server simply broadcasts it back out to everyone on the topic. The broadcasted payload can include anything: strings, numbers, nested maps, even serialized structures.

On the JavaScript side (the client), you push and listen for events like this:

```
channel.push("new_message", {body: "Hi everyone!"})


channel.on("new_message", payload => {

  console.log("Message received:", payload.body)

})
```

This tightly couples user actions (like typing a message) to server-side event handlers without having to manually manage WebSocket low-level APIs.

Key Points about Events:

Events are per-topic.

Payloads are free-form maps.

You can broadcast an event to everyone or reply individually.

PubSub: Broadcast and Subscription Behind the Scenes

When you call `broadcast!/3` inside a channel, Phoenix doesn't just send the message to sockets in memory. It uses an internal **PubSub** system to **publish** the event, and every subscriber (every socket process joined on that topic) **subscribes** to it.

This publish/subscribe model is abstracted for you, but it's powerful and customizable.

Phoenix uses `Phoenix.PubSub` under the hood. You can access it directly outside of channels too.

Example of broadcasting manually:

```
Phoenix.PubSub.broadcast(MyApp.PubSub,
"chat:lobby", %{event: "new_message", body: "System
message"})
```

To receive broadcasts outside a channel, a process can subscribe manually:

```
Phoenix.PubSub.subscribe(MyApp.PubSub,
"chat:lobby")
```

And then listen in `handle_info/2`:

```
def handle_info(%{event: "new_message", body:
body}, socket) do
   {:noreply, update(socket, :messages, fn msgs ->
[body | msgs] end)}
end
```

This is a powerful mechanism because:

Any process—not just channel sockets—can listen for topic updates.

Background tasks, GenServers, LiveViews, and system monitors can all react to PubSub events.

Scaling across nodes or servers is handled automatically (with the right PubSub adapter).

PubSub adapters like `Phoenix.PubSub.Redis` allow you to distribute PubSub events across multiple server nodes using Redis, enabling true horizontal scalability.

Practical Real-World Example: Live Notifications

Let's build a real-time notifications feature.

When something happens (like a new comment on a user's post), you want to push a notification to that user.

First, structure the topic per user:

```
"user:#{user_id}:notifications"
```

When the user connects, they join their notification topic:

```
def join("user:" <> user_id <> ":notifications",
_params, socket) do
```

```
    {:ok, socket}
end
```

On the server, when a new comment is created:

```
Phoenix.PubSub.broadcast(
  MyApp.PubSub,
  "user:42:notifications",
  %{event: "new_notification", message: "You have a
new comment!"}
)
```

If the user is connected to `"user:42:notifications"`, they immediately receive the event, and their UI updates without polling or manual refreshing.

On the client:

```
channel.on("new_notification", payload => {
  alert(payload.message)
})
```

This simple pattern can power notifications, friend requests, order updates, collaborative document edits, or even online presence systems.

Security and Access Control

Because topics are just strings, it's important to control who can join sensitive topics.

In your `join/3`, verify user identity:

```
def join("user:" <> user_id, _params, socket) do
  if user_id == to_string(socket.assigns.user_id)
do
    {:ok, socket}
  else
    {:error, %{reason: "unauthorized"}}
  end
end
```

Never trust client-side data blindly. Always enforce server-side authorization.

Topics, events, and PubSub are the trio that makes Phoenix's real-time system flexible and powerful. You organize communication with topics, define interactions with events, and leverage PubSub to distribute those messages safely and scalably.

Presence and State Synchronization

When you start building real-time applications with Phoenix Channels, one challenge quickly emerges: how do you keep track of users who are connected to a topic? How do you know when they join, leave, or change something about their session? How do you synchronize this information safely, even across multiple servers?

Phoenix answers these questions with **Presence**.

Phoenix Presence is a built-in module designed to track information about connected clients. It handles the heavy lifting of **who is connected**, **what metadata they carry**, and **how to synchronize state changes across nodes**. Presence abstracts the complexity of tracking users, ensuring fault tolerance, and broadcasting changes efficiently.

Setting Up Phoenix Presence

First, you need to define a Presence module for your application.

```
# lib/my_app_web/presence.ex

defmodule MyAppWeb.Presence do

  use Phoenix.Presence,

    otp_app: :my_app,

    pubsub_server: MyApp.PubSub

end
```

This module wraps all the logic for tracking and syncing presences. It uses your app's PubSub system to distribute presence information.

You must also add Presence to your supervision tree:

```
# lib/my_app/application.ex
children = [
  ...,
```

```
    MyAppWeb.Presence
]
```

With this setup, Presence is running and ready to track user connections.

Tracking Users on a Topic

Inside your channel, once a user successfully joins a topic, you can start tracking their presence.

Here's a simple example from a chat room channel:

```
def join("chat:lobby", _payload, socket) do
  send(self(), :after_join)
  {:ok, socket}
end

def handle_info(:after_join, socket) do
  MyAppWeb.Presence.track(
    socket.channel_pid,
    "chat:lobby",
    socket.assigns.user_id,
    %{online_at: System.system_time(:second)}
  )

  push(socket, "presence_state",
MyAppWeb.Presence.list("chat:lobby"))
  {:noreply, socket}
end
```

In handle_info/2, we use Presence.track/4 to associate a user ID with a topic and some metadata, such as the time they joined.

Then, we immediately push the current presence state down to the client so it can render who is already online.

Parameters for Presence.track/4:

socket.channel_pid: the unique process ID of the connected socket.

Topic: the topic string (e.g., "chat:lobby").

Key: typically the user ID (should be unique).

Metadata: any information you want to attach (maps).

Handling Presence Events on the Client

The Phoenix JavaScript client provides tools to easily manage presence information.

You listen for two special events:

"presence_state" — The full presence list when you join.

"presence_diff" — Incremental updates as users join or leave.

Example JavaScript:

```javascript
import {Presence} from "phoenix"

let presences = {}

channel.on("presence_state", state => {
  presences = Presence.syncState(presences, state)
  renderOnlineUsers(presences)
})

channel.on("presence_diff", diff => {
  presences = Presence.syncDiff(presences, diff)
  renderOnlineUsers(presences)
})

function renderOnlineUsers(presences) {
  let userList = Presence.list(presences, (id,
{metas: [first]}) => {
    return `<li>${id} - online since ${new
Date(first.online_at *
1000).toLocaleTimeString()}</li>`
  }).join("")

  document.getElementById("users").innerHTML =
`<ul>${userList}</ul>`
}
```

This approach is efficient:

Presence.syncState merges the full state initially.

Presence.syncDiff applies only the changes later (joins, leaves, metadata updates).

You never have to manually figure out who left or who joined. Presence and PubSub handle all that complexity under the hood.

Tracking Metadata Changes

Presence doesn't just tell you who is online—it can track changes to metadata too.

Suppose you want to indicate whether users are typing:

When a user starts typing:

```
MyAppWeb.Presence.update(socket, "chat:lobby",
socket.assigns.user_id, %{typing: true})
```

When they stop:

```
MyAppWeb.Presence.update(socket, "chat:lobby",
socket.assigns.user_id, %{typing: false})
```

The "`presence_diff`" event will deliver this metadata update to all connected clients, and you can react accordingly.

In your render function on the client:

```
Presence.list(presences, (id, {metas: [first]}) =>
{
  if (first.typing) {
    return `<li>${id} is typing...</li>`
  } else {
    return `<li>${id}</li>`
  }
})
```

This enables live "user is typing…" indicators with no custom infrastructure.

Handling Disconnects Automatically

When a client disconnects, Phoenix automatically removes their tracked presence.

If the client reconnects (for example, after losing internet temporarily), they rejoin the topic, re-track, and the client sees the updated `"presence_state"` and `"presence_diff"` events without you writing manual reconnect logic.

This resilience is built into Presence, leveraging the fact that every channel connection is its own supervised BEAM process. When the process dies, Presence knows the user is gone.

Presence in Distributed Systems

When you have multiple servers (multiple Phoenix nodes), Presence still works.

Here's how:

Each server tracks presences locally.

Presence uses PubSub to synchronize presence diffs across nodes.

Diffs are merged intelligently without duplications or stale data.

This means a user connected to node A will correctly appear to users on node B without extra configuration.

If you use something like Redis for PubSub, messages are broadcast through Redis and synchronized to all Phoenix nodes globally.

This is why Phoenix Presence scales so well out of the box—you don't have to worry about complicated distributed consensus protocols. It's handled for you.

Real-World Example: Collaborative Editing

A classic use case is a collaborative document editor.

Each document could have a topic like `"doc:42"`.

Each user who opens the document joins that topic.

Presence tracks users along with their current cursor position or editing state.

Every cursor move or editing action updates metadata.

Clients listen to `"presence_diff"` and update the shared UI accordingly.

117

You achieve real-time collaboration with near-zero lag, full user tracking, and no expensive polling.

Phoenix Presence is one of the strongest tools available for building real-time applications. It simplifies the complex task of tracking connected users, updating client state, and scaling across servers. Presence helps you:

Track users and their metadata

Synchronize changes in real time

Handle disconnects automatically

Scale reliably across multiple nodes

You no longer need to manually manage connection state, heartbeats, or reconnections. Phoenix and Presence handle all of it, freeing you to focus on building better features for your users.

Scaling Channel Applications

Phoenix Channels are built on the Erlang VM (BEAM), which was designed for building fault-tolerant and distributed systems. This gives you a solid foundation for scaling real-time features, but understanding how to **intentionally design for scale** is still crucial—especially as your user base grows from hundreds to thousands or millions of concurrent connections.

When a client joins a Phoenix Channel, a new lightweight BEAM process is created for that socket. This process:

Is supervised and isolated

Manages its own state

Communicates over a persistent WebSocket

Subscribes to a topic (or multiple topics)

This process-per-socket model allows your system to handle many thousands of connections concurrently because the BEAM is optimized for handling lightweight processes. You're not allocating OS threads or processes—you're creating actors that run with minimal overhead.

On a well-provisioned machine, a single Phoenix node can easily handle 100,000 concurrent connections.

That said, the number of connections is not the only metric that matters. The **rate of events** (messages in and out), **volume of data**, and **complexity of per-user logic** all influence performance.

Distributing PubSub Across Multiple Nodes

By default, Phoenix uses a local PubSub adapter (`Phoenix.PubSub.PG2` or `Phoenix.PubSub.ETS`) which is fine for single-node deployments. But when you run multiple Phoenix servers, you need a distributed PubSub system that synchronizes broadcasts and Presence data across all nodes.

You can switch to the Redis adapter for this:

Add the dependency:

```
{:phoenix_pubsub_redis, "~> 3.0"}
```

Then configure it:

```
config :my_app, MyApp.PubSub,
  adapter: Phoenix.PubSub.Redis,
  url: "redis://localhost:6379"
```

Redis acts as a central event bus. All your Phoenix nodes publish and subscribe through it, ensuring broadcasts reach all clients regardless of which server they're connected to.

This setup works great for:

Sticky session deployments (same client always hits same node)

Load-balanced, containerized apps (Fly.io, Kubernetes, etc.)

Real-time systems with high fan-out (1 event → many receivers)

Session Stickiness and Load Balancing

Because each WebSocket connection is tied to a process in memory, it's essential that a client always connects to the same node while that socket is alive. This is known as a **sticky session**.

Without stickiness, the WebSocket connection can break on each request or reconnect, interrupting real-time behavior.

You can achieve stickiness with:

NGINX with IP hash or session cookie routing

Load balancers like HAProxy or Envoy with sticky connection policies

Platforms like Fly.io, Gigalixir, or Heroku which provide built-in support

Sticky sessions aren't required forever, though. If you're using distributed PubSub and offloading state (to Redis, ETS, or a database), your app can tolerate non-sticky reconnections.

Keeping Socket State Minimal

Each socket process can hold assigns just like a LiveView. But to scale efficiently, you should minimize what you store in memory.

Bad:

```
assign(socket, :recent_messages,
fetch_chat_history(room_id))
```

Good:

```
assign(socket, :room_id, room_id)
```

Then load history only when needed, or cache it outside the socket process.

This keeps your socket process lightweight and makes recovery faster in case of failure.

Offloading Work and Avoiding Bottlenecks

A common mistake is putting too much computation or IO directly inside the channel or event handler.

Avoid this:

```elixir
def handle_in("create_invoice", params, socket) do
  # Slow DB calls
  invoice = MyApp.Billing.create_invoice(params)
  {:reply, {:ok, invoice}, socket}
end
```

Instead, delegate:

```elixir
def handle_in("create_invoice", params, socket) do

  Task.start(fn ->
MyApp.Billing.create_invoice(params) end)

  {:noreply, socket}

end
```

Or push it to a GenServer:

```elixir
def handle_in("enqueue_job", params, socket) do

  MyApp.JobQueue.enqueue(params)

  {:noreply, socket}

end
```

This pattern helps prevent bottlenecks and lets you manage concurrency more explicitly.

Monitoring Channel Performance with Telemetry

Phoenix Channels emit telemetry events you can hook into to measure performance:

```elixir
:telemetry.attach(
  "channel-logger",
  [:phoenix, :channel, :join],
  fn event, measurements, metadata, _config ->
    IO.inspect({event, measurements, metadata})
  end,
  nil
)
```

You can measure:

Join times

Event throughput

Message size

Broadcast frequency

Feed this into metrics dashboards (Grafana, Datadog, Prometheus) to observe traffic patterns and bottlenecks in real time.

Designing for Fan-Out

If one message must reach thousands of clients, your system must be efficient at **fan-out**.

Avoid re-broadcasting manually to each socket. Instead, publish once via PubSub:

```
Phoenix.PubSub.broadcast(MyApp.PubSub,
"chat:lobby", %{event: "new_message", body:
"Welcome!"})
```

Every socket subscribed to `"chat:lobby"` receives it instantly, even across nodes. Phoenix handles message distribution through its PubSub backend (ETS or Redis), making fan-out scalable by design.

If you need to send messages based on conditions (e.g., user preferences), you can use per-user topics or Presence metadata to target users appropriately.

Horizontal Scaling in Kubernetes or Fly.io

For full-scale deployments:

Use **Redis PubSub** to synchronize messages.

Deploy multiple replicas of your Phoenix app.

Ensure sticky sessions using platform-specific options:

`fly.toml`: use `[[services.ports]]` with `handlers = ["tls", "http"]`

Kubernetes: use `sessionAffinity: ClientIP` in your Service definition

Use `libcluster` to allow Erlang nodes to auto-discover each other and share Presence data directly (optional but powerful).

Place business logic in GenServers or background workers, not channel processes.

This architecture lets you scale from one to many nodes with confidence.

Real-World Example: Live Sports Scores

Suppose you're building a live sports dashboard where:

Each user is subscribed to their favorite teams

Scores update in real time

Users can send cheers or emoji reactions

You'd organize your topics like:

```
"scores:team_arsenal"

"scores:team_chelsea"
```

Each team's scoring service (via a worker, task, or API feed) broadcasts updates:

```
Phoenix.PubSub.broadcast(MyApp.PubSub,
"scores:team_arsenal", %{event: "score_update",
score: "2 - 1"})
```

Every client watching that game receives the event instantly.

You track users using Presence:

```
MyAppWeb.Presence.track(

  socket.channel_pid,

  "scores:team_arsenal",

  socket.assigns.user_id,

  %{emoji: nil}
```

)

When a user reacts, update metadata. When a goal is scored, everyone sees the live response.

This architecture supports:

Per-topic fan-out

Distributed state sync

Reactions without full page reloads

And it scales to thousands of concurrent viewers with minimal effort.

Phoenix Channels scale because they're backed by lightweight processes, a flexible PubSub system, and a clear separation between real-time transport and business logic. To scale well:

Use Redis PubSub in multi-node setups

Minimize in-memory socket state

Use sticky sessions where needed

Delegate heavy computation outside the channel

Monitor with Telemetry

Test for fan-out performance under load

With these practices, you can confidently build chat apps, dashboards, multiplayer games, collaborative editors, and live event platforms that handle real-time demands at scale.

Chapter 7: Background Jobs and Asynchronous Processing with Oban

As you build more complex Phoenix applications, you'll quickly encounter tasks that should not happen inside a user's web request. Sending emails, processing uploads, syncing with external APIs, generating PDFs, crunching analytics data—these operations can be slow or unreliable. Performing them during a live HTTP or WebSocket event would slow down the user's experience and risk crashing the process if something goes wrong.

The best way to handle these operations is to offload them to a **background job**. This way, the web layer stays fast and responsive, while heavy work happens asynchronously, with retries and fault tolerance.

Phoenix does not ship with a background job library by default, but the Elixir ecosystem offers a powerful, production-ready tool for this: **Oban**.

Oban brings background jobs to Elixir applications using the reliability of PostgreSQL as its data store. It's robust, scalable, transactional, and integrates cleanly with Phoenix and Ecto.

Introduction to Oban

In web applications, there are many tasks that you don't want to run directly inside a user's request. Things like sending confirmation emails, resizing images, creating reports, synchronizing data with external services, or generating invoices can all take time and resources. If you perform them synchronously during a live request, you risk slowing down the response or even crashing the server under load.

Instead of forcing the user to wait, the best practice is to offload that work to a background job system. In Elixir and Phoenix applications, one of the best tools available for this is **Oban**.

Oban is a robust, production-grade background job processing library for Elixir. It is built around PostgreSQL, meaning it doesn't require any extra infrastructure like Redis or RabbitMQ. All job information—such as queued tasks, execution state, retries, and scheduling—is stored safely in your existing database, with full transactional support. It scales cleanly across multiple servers and integrates easily into the supervision tree of any Elixir application.

Oban stands out because it fits the philosophy of the BEAM and Elixir ecosystems perfectly: fault-tolerance, scalability, and explicit concurrency. Here are some reasons why developers trust Oban for background jobs:

Reliability: Jobs are inserted into the database inside transactions, ensuring no jobs are lost even if the app crashes.

Persistence: Jobs survive crashes and reboots since they live in PostgreSQL.

Automatic Retries: Jobs that fail are retried automatically with customizable backoff strategies.

Concurrency: You can control how many jobs run at once per queue.

Scheduled Jobs: You can schedule jobs to run later, not just immediately.

Visibility: Oban offers a web dashboard for inspecting running, scheduled, completed, or failed jobs.

Clustering: Oban supports distributed execution across multiple application nodes with no extra coordination service required.

Oban provides a comprehensive toolkit without forcing you to adopt a complicated new service architecture. If you already have a Phoenix and PostgreSQL stack, you can start using Oban immediately.

Installing and Setting Up Oban

Let's walk through setting up Oban step-by-step.

First, add Oban to your project dependencies:

```
# mix.exs
defp deps do
  [
    {:oban, "~> 2.14"}
  ]
end
```

Fetch the new dependency:

```
mix deps.get
```

Next, you must configure Oban in your `config/config.exs`:

```
# config/config.exs

config :my_app, Oban,

  repo: MyApp.Repo,

  plugins: [Oban.Plugins.Pruner],

  queues: [default: 10]
```

Here you tell Oban which Ecto repository to use (`MyApp.Repo`), set up plugins (like the **Pruner** which cleans up old jobs), and define queues. Queues are where your jobs are executed. You can configure different queues with different levels of concurrency.

Now, add Oban to your supervision tree:

```
# lib/my_app/application.ex
children = [
  MyApp.Repo,
  {Oban, Application.fetch_env!(:my_app, Oban)}
]
```

This ensures Oban runs as a supervised process, monitoring and executing background jobs.

Before you can use Oban, you need a database table to store jobs. Generate a migration:

```
mix ecto.gen.migration add_oban_jobs_table
```

Inside the migration file, call the built-in helper:

```
defmodule MyApp.Repo.Migrations.AddObanJobsTable do
  use Ecto.Migration

  def up, do: Oban.Migrations.up()
  def down, do: Oban.Migrations.down()
end
```

Run the migration:

```
mix ecto.migrate
```

Now your database is ready to hold jobs.

At this point, Oban is fully integrated into your application and ready to handle background work.

Basic Concepts in Oban

Workers

In Oban, a "job" is defined by a **worker** module. A worker defines what the job does when it executes.

Example:

```
defmodule MyApp.Workers.WelcomeEmailWorker do
  use Oban.Worker, queue: :default, max_attempts: 5

  @impl Oban.Worker
  def perform(%Oban.Job{args: %{"user_id" =>
user_id}}) do
    user = MyApp.Accounts.get_user!(user_id)
    MyApp.Mailer.deliver_welcome_email(user)
    :ok
  end
end
```

This defines a job that sends a welcome email to a user.

Enqueuing Jobs

Once a worker is defined, you can enqueue a job like this:

```
%{"user_id" => user.id}

|> MyApp.Workers.WelcomeEmailWorker.new()

|> Oban.insert()
```

Or shorter:

```
Oban.insert(MyApp.Workers.WelcomeEmailWorker.new(%{
"user_id" => user.id}))
```

The job is written to the database and will be picked up by Oban for execution, obeying your configured concurrency limits.

Example: Offloading Email Delivery

When a new user registers, instead of blocking the response while you send a welcome email, you enqueue a background job:

Inside your registration controller:

```
def register_user(params) do
  {:ok, user} = Accounts.create_user(params)

Oban.insert(MyApp.Workers.WelcomeEmailWorker.new(%{
"user_id" => user.id}))
  {:ok, user}
end
```

The user sees instant feedback ("Account created!") without waiting for the email service to respond. Meanwhile, the WelcomeEmailWorker handles sending the email in the background.

If the job fails (say, because the SMTP server is temporarily unavailable), Oban retries it automatically according to its retry policy.

Real-World Scenarios Where Oban Excels

Sending emails without blocking user interaction

Uploading or processing large files asynchronously

Integrating with payment gateways and processing delayed webhooks

Generating and sending PDF invoices after purchases

Cleaning up expired sessions, caches, or old records

Polling external APIs regularly

Performing data migration tasks during deployments

In all these cases, Oban ensures that work is reliable, transactional, fault-tolerant, and efficient.

Oban is a reliable, production-grade background job system for Elixir and Phoenix applications. It leverages PostgreSQL for persistence and fault tolerance, integrates naturally into your existing app structure, and gives you the tools you need to manage asynchronous work cleanly and safely.

Defining, Enqueuing, and Executing Jobs

Once Oban is properly installed and configured in your application, the next step is understanding how to define a job, enqueue it with the right arguments, and allow Oban to execute it safely and reliably. This is the essential workflow behind background processing.

A **job** in Oban is defined by a module that implements the `Oban.Worker` behaviour. This module is responsible for declaring the type of work to perform, defining execution options like which queue it should run in, and then actually executing that work when the job runs.

Defining a Job

Start by creating a worker module. Every job in Oban starts with a module that uses `Oban.Worker`.

Here's a simple job that sends a welcome email to a user:

```
defmodule MyApp.Workers.WelcomeEmailWorker do
  use Oban.Worker,
    queue: :default,
    max_attempts: 5,
    tags: ["emails", "welcome"]

  @impl Oban.Worker
  def perform(%Oban.Job{args: %{"user_id" =>
user_id}}) do
    user = MyApp.Accounts.get_user!(user_id)
    MyApp.Mailer.deliver_welcome_email(user)
    :ok
  end
end
```

Here's what this definition tells Oban:

The job will run in the :default queue.

It will retry up to 5 times if it fails.

It tags the job for logging or monitoring purposes.

The perform/1 function is where the actual business logic happens. Oban passes in an %Oban.Job{} struct that includes the job's arguments and metadata.

You should always return one of the following:

:ok if the job succeeds.

{:error, reason} or raise an error if the job fails (Oban will retry).

{:discard, reason} if you want to skip retrying and permanently fail the job.

Avoid returning custom formats. Oban expects clear signals for success or failure.

Enqueuing a Job

Once you've defined a worker, you can enqueue jobs from anywhere in your application—controllers, LiveViews, contexts, or even other jobs.

To enqueue the WelcomeEmailWorker, pass the necessary arguments in a map:

```
%{"user_id" => user.id}
|> MyApp.Workers.WelcomeEmailWorker.new()
|> Oban.insert()
```

Or directly:

```
Oban.insert(MyApp.Workers.WelcomeEmailWorker.new(%{
"user_id" => user.id}))
```

The `%{"user_id" => user.id}` part must be a **map with string keys**. Oban serializes the data to JSON and stores it in the `args` column of the database.

This job is now persisted in the `oban_jobs` table. Oban's supervision tree picks it up and dispatches it to an available worker process for execution.

If you need to enqueue a job from within an Ecto transaction (like when creating a new user), you can do it safely like this:

```
Repo.transaction(fn ->
  user = Repo.insert!(%User{name: "Ada"})

Oban.insert!(MyApp.Workers.WelcomeEmailWorker.new(%
{"user_id" => user.id}))
end)
```

This guarantees the job will only be inserted if the user was successfully created.

Customizing Job Execution

Oban gives you fine-grained control over how each job runs. Let's explore some useful options.

Named Queues

You can define multiple queues in your configuration:

```
config :my_app, Oban,

  queues: [default: 10, mailers: 5, video: 2]
```

Then in your worker:

```
use Oban.Worker, queue: :mailers
```

This routes the job to the `:mailers` queue, which allows up to 5 concurrent jobs.

Retrying Failed Jobs

By default, jobs retry up to 20 times with exponential backoff. You can customize the retry count:

```
use Oban.Worker, max_attempts: 3
```

To trigger a retry, return an error or raise an exception:

```
def perform(%Oban.Job{} = job) do
  case send_email(job.args) do
    :ok -> :ok
    {:error, reason} -> {:error, reason}
  end
end
```

If the job hits its retry limit, it's marked as `discarded`.

Disabling Retries

If a job should not retry on failure:

```
use Oban.Worker, max_attempts: 1
```

Discarding Jobs Manually

Sometimes you want to explicitly discard a job without retrying:

```
def perform(%Oban.Job{args: %{"email" => email}})
do
  if valid_email?(email) do
    deliver(email)
    :ok
  else
    {:discard, "invalid email"}
  end
end
```

Discarded jobs appear in the Oban dashboard but are not retried.

Monitoring Jobs in Oban Web UI

Oban offers a paid web dashboard called **Oban Web**, which gives you visibility into:

Active jobs

Completed jobs

Failed jobs

Scheduled and retrying jobs

With it, you can retry, cancel, or inspect jobs. It integrates with Phoenix and gives you a detailed view of how your background processing system is behaving in production.

Even without Oban Web, you can use SQL queries or build a basic dashboard to read from the `oban_jobs` table. For example:

```
Repo.all(from j in Oban.Job, where: j.state ==
"available", order_by: [desc: j.inserted_at])
```

This shows all pending jobs waiting to be processed.

Testing Oban Jobs

Testing jobs is important. You can write unit tests for the `perform/1` function directly:

```
test "sends welcome email" do
  user = insert(:user)

  assert :ok =

MyApp.Workers.WelcomeEmailWorker.perform(%Oban.Job{
args: %{"user_id" => user.id}})
end
```

You can also test that jobs are enqueued properly:

```
test "enqueues welcome email" do
  user = insert(:user)

  {:ok, job} =

Oban.insert(MyApp.Workers.WelcomeEmailWorker.new(%{
"user_id" => user.id}))

  assert job.args["user_id"] == user.id
end
```

To simulate execution in tests, you can run jobs immediately using `Oban.Testing.perform_job/2`.

With Oban, defining, enqueuing, and executing jobs is clear and safe. You write plain Elixir modules, enqueue jobs with simple maps, and let Oban take care of persistence, concurrency, and retries. It integrates smoothly with Ecto, supports advanced scheduling and queueing strategies, and handles failure in a way that's consistent with Elixir's philosophy of fault tolerance.

This foundation lets you build responsive, reliable systems where the user interface stays snappy, and heavy tasks are processed independently in the background.

Handling Retries, Failures, and Scheduled Jobs

No matter how carefully you build your application, real-world systems are full of unpredictable factors: API calls can fail, email servers can go down, databases can lock up under load. When you push work into background jobs, you gain an opportunity to deal with these issues gracefully. A well-designed job system doesn't just process tasks—it retries failures intelligently, discards jobs that cannot be completed, and schedules work for the right moment.

Oban gives you robust, built-in strategies for **retries**, **failures**, and **scheduling**. Handling these correctly ensures your application stays reliable even under adverse conditions.

When a job fails in Oban—because it raises an exception, returns an error tuple (`{:error, reason}`), or crashes—it doesn't disappear. Instead, it enters a retrying state.

Oban uses a **backoff strategy** to determine how long to wait before trying the job again. By default, this is an exponential backoff with jitter (randomness), so retries don't hammer your system all at once.

Here's a simple worker that might need retries:

```
defmodule MyApp.Workers.SendInvoiceWorker do
  use Oban.Worker, queue: :billing, max_attempts: 5

  @impl Oban.Worker
  def perform(%Oban.Job{args: %{"invoice_id" =>
id}}) do
    case MyApp.Billing.send_invoice(id) do
```

```
      :ok -> :ok
      {:error, _reason} -> {:error, "Invoice
sending failed"}
    end
  end
end
```

If `send_invoice/1` returns an error, the job will be retried automatically, up to `max_attempts` times. After the maximum retries are exhausted, the job moves to the "`discarded`" state.

The retries happen progressively:

First retry: after a few seconds

Next retry: after a bit longer

Subsequent retries: further apart

This protects your system from being flooded by repeated failures.

Customizing Retry Behavior

You can fully control how retries behave by customizing the backoff strategy.

For example, to make retries happen exactly 10 minutes apart:

```
defmodule MyApp.Workers.CriticalWorker do

  use Oban.Worker, backoff:
& __MODULE__.custom_backoff/1


  def custom_backoff(attempt) do

    attempt * 600  # seconds (10 minutes per
attempt)

  end

end
```

You can also reduce the number of retry attempts by setting `max_attempts: 3` if needed.

If a failure is unrecoverable (such as invalid input), you can skip retries entirely by returning a {:discard, reason} tuple inside perform/1:

```
def perform(%Oban.Job{args: %{"file" =>
file_path}}) do
  if File.exists?(file_path) do
    process_file(file_path)
    :ok
  else
    {:discard, "File not found"}
  end
end
```

Discarded jobs are recorded for audit purposes but will not be retried.

Handling Job Failures

Failures are not an exception to background processing; they are a normal part of building distributed systems. Oban helps you handle them explicitly.

When a job permanently fails (after exhausting retries), it moves to the "discarded" state.

You can build tooling to observe or act on discarded jobs:

Example query to find discarded jobs:

```
Oban.Job

|> where([j], j.state == "discarded")

|> MyApp.Repo.all()
```

If you use **Oban Web** (the commercial dashboard), you can see, retry, cancel, or inspect failed jobs visually.

You can also set up alerts or logging for failed jobs:

```
:telemetry.attach(
  "oban-failure-logger",
  [:oban, :job, :exception],
  fn event, measurements, metadata, _config ->
    Logger.error("""
    Oban job failed:
```

```
      Worker: #{metadata.worker}
      Args: #{inspect(metadata.args)}
      Error: #{inspect(measurements.error)}
    """)
  end,
  nil
)
```

This ensures that you're aware when things go wrong instead of finding out later through angry user reports.

Scheduling Jobs for Future Execution

Not all work needs to happen immediately. Sometimes you want to schedule jobs to run **later**.

Oban makes scheduling extremely easy.

Here's how you schedule a job to run in 1 hour:

```
MyApp.Workers.EmailReminderWorker.new(%{"user_id"
=> user.id}, schedule_in: 3600)

|> Oban.insert()
```

Or to run at a specific datetime:

```
scheduled_time = DateTime.add(DateTime.utc_now(),
3600)

MyApp.Workers.EmailReminderWorker.new(%{"user_id"
=> user.id}, scheduled_at: scheduled_time)
|> Oban.insert()
```

Scheduled jobs are inserted into the database immediately but remain inactive until the scheduled time is reached.

Oban's supervisor process periodically checks for scheduled jobs whose time has arrived and enqueues them automatically for execution.

Practical Example: Welcome Email Reminder

Suppose you want to send a reminder email if a user hasn't completed onboarding within 24 hours.

When the user signs up:

```
Oban.insert(MyApp.Workers.WelcomeReminderWorker.new
(%{"user_id" => user.id}, schedule_in: 86400))
```

Inside the worker:

```
defmodule MyApp.Workers.WelcomeReminderWorker do
  use Oban.Worker,, queue: :mailers

  @impl Oban.Worker
  def perform(%Oban.Job{args: %{"user_id" =>
user_id}}) do
    user = MyApp.Accounts.get_user!(user_id)

    unless user.onboarded? do
      MyApp.Mailer.send_onboarding_reminder(user)
    end

    :ok
  end
end
```

If the user completes onboarding before the job runs, you can simply **cancel** the job using the job ID or unique constraint keys, depending on how you inserted it.

Best Practices for Retries, Failures, and Scheduling

Treat failure as normal, not an exception.

Log or monitor discarded jobs for operational awareness.

Design idempotent jobs that can safely run multiple times.

Discard jobs explicitly when you know retrying won't help (e.g., invalid email addresses).

Use scheduling for non-urgent workflows like reminders or batch operations.

Keep your `perform/1` logic small—if it gets complex, delegate to context modules.

Handling retries, failures, and scheduled jobs properly is what makes your background processing system resilient and trustworthy. With Oban:

Retries happen automatically with backoff strategies.

Failures are recorded, observable, and manageable.

Jobs can be scheduled into the future with just a few lines of code.

Your Phoenix application becomes more fault-tolerant, responsive, and able to gracefully recover from the inevitable issues that arise in real-world systems.

Real-World Use Cases for Background Processing

Background jobs are not just an optimization—they are often the only practical way to keep your application responsive and scalable as your features grow. Any time you have work that's slow, external, failure-prone, resource-intensive, or can be deferred without blocking a user's experience, it belongs in a background process.

With Oban, integrating background jobs into a Phoenix or Elixir application is not just efficient—it's a natural fit. You're building on a fault-tolerant runtime with strong concurrency support and transactional data guarantees.

Email Delivery and Notification Systems

Email is a core feature for many applications—welcome emails, password resets, transactional updates, promotional newsletters. However, sending an email is slow. It usually involves contacting an SMTP server, which can delay your HTTP response.

Instead of making the user wait for an email to be sent, you enqueue the work.

Worker:

```
defmodule MyApp.Workers.SendEmailWorker do
  use Oban.Worker, queue: :mailers

  @impl Oban.Worker
  def perform(%Oban.Job{args: %{"user_id" =>
user_id, "template" => template}}) do
```

```
      user = MyApp.Accounts.get_user!(user_id)
      MyApp.Mailer.send_email(user, template)    .
      :ok
   end
end
```

Enqueue in controller:

```
def create(conn, params) do
  {:ok, user} = Accounts.register_user(params)

  %{"user_id" => user.id, "template" => "welcome"}
  |> MyApp.Workers.SendEmailWorker.new()
  |> Oban.insert()

  conn
  |> put_flash(:info, "User created successfully")
  |> redirect(to: Routes.page_path(conn, :index))
end
```

This keeps the signup flow instant while ensuring the email is delivered reliably.

Video and File Processing

If your app lets users upload videos, images, or large files, you often need to process these files—resize images, transcode videos, extract thumbnails. These operations can be CPU-intensive and slow.

Worker:

```
defmodule MyApp.Workers.ProcessVideoWorker do
  use Oban.Worker, queue: :media

  @impl Oban.Worker
  def perform(%Oban.Job{args: %{"video_id" => id}})
do
    video = MyApp.Media.get_video!(id)
    MyApp.Media.transcode_video(video)
    :ok
  end
end
```

When a video upload completes:

```
Oban.insert(MyApp.Workers.ProcessVideoWorker.new(%{
"video_id" => video.id}))
```

Users can continue browsing while their video processes asynchronously in the background.

External API Synchronization

Many systems depend on third-party APIs—payment processors like Stripe, CRM systems, or external data feeds. These external calls can be slow or unreliable.

Instead of making synchronous API calls that block a user, enqueue a background job to sync data later.

Worker:

```
defmodule MyApp.Workers.SyncStripeCustomerWorker do
  use Oban.Worker, queue: :sync

  @impl Oban.Worker
  def perform(%Oban.Job{args: %{"customer_id" =>
stripe_id}}) do
    case Stripe.API.fetch_customer(stripe_id) do
      {:ok, customer_data} ->

MyApp.Billing.update_customer_from_stripe(customer_
data)
        :ok

      {:error, _reason} ->
        {:error, "Failed to sync Stripe customer"}
    end
  end
end
```

Enqueue:

```
Oban.insert(MyApp.Workers.SyncStripeCustomerWorker.
new(%{"customer_id" => stripe_id}))
```

If the Stripe API is down temporarily, the job will retry automatically later.

Scheduled Reminders and Notifications

Suppose you want to send a reminder email or notification 24 hours after a user signs up if they haven't completed a task.

You can schedule a job when the user signs up:

```
Oban.insert(
  MyApp.Workers.OnboardingReminderWorker.new(
    %{"user_id" => user.id},
    schedule_in: 86_400  # 24 hours
  )
)
```

Worker:

```
defmodule MyApp.Workers.OnboardingReminderWorker do
  use Oban.Worker, queue: :mailers

  @impl Oban.Worker
  def perform(%Oban.Job{args: %{"user_id" =>
user_id}}) do
    user = MyApp.Accounts.get_user!(user_id)

    unless user.completed_onboarding? do
      MyApp.Mailer.send_onboarding_reminder(user)
    end

    :ok
  end
end
```

This ensures timely engagement without needing a complex scheduler service.

Data Cleanup and Maintenance Tasks

Over time, applications accumulate old data—expired sessions, abandoned carts, stale records. These need to be cleaned up regularly.

You can schedule recurring cleanup jobs using Oban's Cron plugin.

Configuration:

```
config :my_app, Oban,
  plugins: [
```

```
    {Oban.Plugins.Cron, crontab: [
      {"0 3 * * *",
MyApp.Workers.CleanupSessionsWorker} # every day at
3 AM
    ]}
  ]
```

Worker:

```
defmodule MyApp.Workers.CleanupSessionsWorker do
  use Oban.Worker, queue: :maintenance

  @impl Oban.Worker
  def perform(_job) do
    MyApp.Sessions.expire_old_sessions()
    :ok
  end
end
```

This automates background maintenance without affecting live user traffic.

Push Notifications and In-App Alerts

If your app supports push notifications or live alerts, background jobs ensure they are sent reliably even if the frontend client is offline when an event occurs.

Worker:

```
defmodule MyApp.Workers.SendPushNotificationWorker
do
  use Oban.Worker, queue: :notifications

  @impl Oban.Worker
  def perform(%Oban.Job{args: %{"device_id" =>
device_id, "message" => message}}) do
    MyApp.Push.send_notification(device_id,
message)
    :ok
  end
end
```

Usage:

```
Oban.insert(MyApp.Workers.SendPushNotificationWorke
r.new(%{
  "device_id" => user.device_id,
  "message" => "Your order has shipped!"
}))
```

Users get notified reliably without delay, even if external push services are temporarily slow.

Best Practices When Designing Background Workflows

Make your workers **idempotent**. If a job runs twice, it should not cause problems.

Log errors and monitor retries to catch persistent failures early.

Control concurrency using queue configuration to avoid overloading external services.

Use job arguments carefully. Pass only necessary lightweight data (like IDs), not large payloads.

Batch work when appropriate—sometimes it's more efficient to process multiple items in one job.

Background processing unlocks a whole new level of responsiveness, reliability, and scalability for your Phoenix applications. With Oban, you can:

Offload slow work like emails and file processing

Handle external API failures gracefully

Schedule work to happen at the right time

Keep your user experience fast and uninterrupted

Automate routine maintenance tasks

You no longer need to build complex manual queues or babysit fragile processes. Background jobs become first-class citizens in your application, managed, retried, and monitored with full reliability.

Chapter 8: Building Fault-Tolerant Systems with OTP

When you start working with Elixir and Phoenix, you quickly realize that you're standing on the shoulders of a very powerful foundation—the BEAM virtual machine and its native support for fault tolerance through OTP (Open Telecom Platform). While you can build useful web applications without understanding OTP deeply, true mastery of Elixir comes when you start designing your own fault-tolerant processes and supervision trees.

OTP gives you the building blocks to write applications that can detect errors, recover from failures automatically, and continue running without interruption. You don't need massive infrastructure or complicated failover tools—you get these capabilities natively by writing correct Elixir code.

GenServers and Supervisors

In Elixir, everything runs as a process—lightweight, isolated, and managed by the BEAM virtual machine. But not all processes are the same. Some are fire-and-forget tasks, others keep long-lived state or handle important workflows. For those that manage internal state or coordinate message passing, Elixir gives you a powerful abstraction: the **GenServer**.

A **GenServer** (short for generic server) is a behaviour module that allows you to create processes which can maintain internal state, handle synchronous and asynchronous messages, and participate in OTP's supervision model.

A **Supervisor**, on the other hand, is responsible for monitoring these GenServers (and other workers). If one crashes, the supervisor restarts it using a well-defined strategy.

What Is a GenServer Really Doing?

At the most basic level, a GenServer is a process that receives messages, updates its state, and replies where necessary. You can send it a `cast` (asynchronous, no reply) or a `call` (synchronous, expects a reply). Under the hood, a GenServer just loops through its internal state and keeps updating it after every message.

Let's implement a simple key-value store in memory using a GenServer.

```elixir
defmodule MyApp.KVStore do
  use GenServer

  # Client API

  def start_link(_opts) do
    GenServer.start_link(__MODULE__, %{}, name:
__MODULE__)
  end

  def put(key, value) do
    GenServer.cast(__MODULE__, {:put, key, value})
  end

  def get(key) do
    GenServer.call(__MODULE__, {:get, key})
  end

  # Server Callbacks

  @impl true
  def init(state) do
    {:ok, state}
  end

  @impl true
  def handle_cast({:put, key, value}, state) do
    {:noreply, Map.put(state, key, value)}
  end

  @impl true
  def handle_call({:get, key}, _from, state) do
    {:reply, Map.get(state, key), state}
  end
end
```

Let's walk through it clearly.

start_link/1 starts the GenServer process and registers it under the module name.

put/2 uses GenServer.cast/2 to send an update command.

`get/1` uses `GenServer.call/2` to retrieve data from the server.

The server holds its internal state as a simple map.

`handle_cast/2` updates state without replying.

`handle_call/3` looks up a key and sends the value back to the caller.

To use it:

```
MyApp.KVStore.start_link([])

MyApp.KVStore.put(:username, "nehemiah")

MyApp.KVStore.get(:username)

# => "nehemiah"
```

Each time you `put`, the internal map is updated. Each time you `get`, the current value is returned—without ever exposing the state directly.

Supervising GenServers

In production, a GenServer can crash—for example, due to a bug, memory exhaustion, or failed external call. Instead of writing manual recovery logic, you use **Supervisors**.

A Supervisor watches your GenServer and restarts it if it crashes.

You can define a supervisor like this:

```
defmodule MyApp.Supervisor do
  use Supervisor

  def start_link(_opts) do
    Supervisor.start_link(__MODULE__, :ok, name:
__MODULE__)
  end

  @impl true
  def init(:ok) do
    children = [
      {MyApp.KVStore, []}
    ]
```

```
    Supervisor.init(children, strategy:
  :one_for_one)
    end
end
```

You tell the supervisor:

Which child modules to start

What strategy to use if one of them crashes

The :one_for_one strategy means "if one child crashes, restart that child only." This is the most common and safest default.

Then, in your app's main module:

```
defmodule MyApp.Application do
  use Application

  @impl true
  def start(_type, _args) do
    children = [
      MyApp.Supervisor
    ]

    opts = [strategy: :one_for_one, name:
MyApp.AppSupervisor]
    Supervisor.start_link(children, opts)
  end
end
```

This completes your supervision tree. If KVStore ever crashes, it will be restarted automatically. If the crash was a fluke (e.g., network blip or bad input), this gives your system resilience with no extra effort.

Real Example: In-Memory Rate Limiter

Let's say you want to build a basic rate limiter that keeps track of how many requests a user has made within a short time frame.

GenServer version:

```
defmodule MyApp.RateLimiter do
```

```elixir
  use GenServer

  @max_requests 10
  @window_seconds 60

  def start_link(_opts) do
    GenServer.start_link(__MODULE__, %{}, name:
__MODULE__)
  end

  def allowed?(user_id) do
    GenServer.call(__MODULE__, {:check, user_id})
  end

  @impl true
  def init(_state), do: {:ok, %{}}

  @impl true
  def handle_call({:check, user_id}, _from, state)
do
    now = System.system_time(:second)
    user_state = Map.get(state, user_id, [])

    updated = [now | Enum.filter(user_state, fn ts
-> now - ts <= @window_seconds end)]

    if length(updated) <= @max_requests do
      {:reply, true, Map.put(state, user_id,
updated)}
    else
      {:reply, false, Map.put(state, user_id,
updated)}
    end
  end
end
```

This is a basic sliding window rate limiter. It works entirely in memory, using timestamps to determine whether a user has exceeded their quota.

You can wire this into your Phoenix controller like:

```elixir
if MyApp.RateLimiter.allowed?(user.id) do
  # proceed
```

```
else
  conn
  |> put_status(:too_many_requests)
  |> json(%{error: "Rate limit exceeded"})
end
```

Even if `RateLimiter` crashes, your supervisor will restart it, and your system continues serving users.

Letting GenServers Crash Gracefully

Don't try to "defend" every possible failure in your GenServer. If you hit unrecoverable state—say, corrupt memory or a poisoned cache—it's better to let the process crash and get restarted than to try to limp along with bad data.

Example:

```
def handle_call(:fail, _from, _state) do
  raise "Intentional failure"
end
```

This causes the GenServer to crash. But if it's under a supervisor, it'll be restarted immediately, typically with a clean state. That's better than masking the error or leaving your process in a half-broken state.

This is known as **"let it crash"**—a core principle in Elixir and Erlang development.

When to Use GenServer vs Other Abstractions

Use a GenServer when:

You need to keep **state** over time

You want to **encapsulate access** to that state

You need to **coordinate access** between multiple processes

You want to **respond to events or timers**

You don't need GenServer for everything. Sometimes, a stateless module or a one-off Task is better. Use GenServers when **persistent process state** makes the logic cleaner and safer.

GenServers and Supervisors are foundational tools for building fault-tolerant systems in Elixir. With them, you can:

Encapsulate and protect mutable state

Design processes that respond to both synchronous and asynchronous messages

Handle errors by letting processes crash and recover safely

Build systems that heal themselves automatically, without needing complex retry logic

Application Structure and Lifecycle

When you build an Elixir application, you are not just writing modules and functions—you are building a structured system that has a clear lifecycle, managed by the BEAM virtual machine and OTP's supervision principles. This lifecycle governs how your application starts, runs, recovers from failures, and shuts down gracefully.

Understanding the **application structure** and **lifecycle** is essential for writing robust, scalable systems in Elixir. It's not something you add at the end; it is baked into how you design and organize your code from the beginning.

The Application Module: Entry Point of Your System

Every Elixir application has an **application module**. This module implements the `Application` behaviour and defines a `start/2` callback.

This module is your main entry point. It's responsible for starting your supervision tree.

Here's a basic application module:

```
defmodule MyApp.Application do
  use Application

  @impl true
  def start(_type, _args) do
    children = [
      MyApp.Repo,
      MyAppWeb.Endpoint,
```

```
      {Oban, Application.fetch_env!(:my_app,
Oban)},
        MyApp.Cache
     ]

     opts = [strategy: :one_for_one, name:
MyApp.Supervisor]
        Supervisor.start_link(children, opts)
   end
end
```

When you start the application (e.g., with `iex -S mix` or in production with `mix release`), this `start/2` function is called.

What happens in this function:

You define a list of children: workers, GenServers, supervision trees, tasks, anything that should be part of your runtime system.

You pass these children into a Supervisor, specifying a supervision strategy (most commonly `:one_for_one`).

You return the result of `Supervisor.start_link/2`, which hooks everything into the OTP runtime.

Without this structure, your application would have no persistence, no fault recovery, and no clean way to manage processes.

What Happens During Startup

Here's a clear picture of the lifecycle:

The BEAM loads your compiled application.

The `start/2` function in your Application module is called.

Your top-level Supervisor starts and begins starting child processes.

Each child process starts (by calling `start_link/1` or similar).

If any child fails to start, the entire tree is taken down, and your application fails to boot cleanly (this is intentional—it prevents partial or broken states).

Because of this strict startup model, you want to be careful that child processes either start successfully or crash immediately, rather than limping along in a bad state.

Structuring Your Supervision Tree

In a production-grade Phoenix app (or any serious Elixir app), your supervision tree should be **layered**, not flat.

You don't want one big supervisor with 50 children. Instead, you want **nested supervisors** that each manage logical groups of related processes.

Example:

```elixir
defmodule MyApp.Application do
  use Application

  @impl true
  def start(_type, _args) do
    children = [
      MyApp.Repo,
      MyAppWeb.Endpoint,
      MyApp.Background.Supervisor,
      MyApp.CacheSupervisor
    ]

    opts = [strategy: :one_for_one, name:
MyApp.Supervisor]
    Supervisor.start_link(children, opts)
  end
end
```

Then you have individual supervisors like:

```elixir
defmodule MyApp.Background.Supervisor do
  use Supervisor

  @impl true
  def start_link(_init_arg) do
    Supervisor.start_link(__MODULE__, :ok, name:
__MODULE__)
  end
```

```elixir
  @impl true
  def init(:ok) do
    children = [
      {Oban, Application.fetch_env!(:my_app,
Oban)},
      MyApp.JobQueue
    ]

    Supervisor.init(children, strategy:
:one_for_one)
  end
end
```

And:

```elixir
defmodule MyApp.CacheSupervisor do
  use Supervisor

  @impl true
  def start_link(_init_arg) do
    Supervisor.start_link(__MODULE__, :ok, name:
__MODULE__)
  end

  @impl true
  def init(:ok) do
    children = [
      MyApp.KVStore,
      MyApp.SessionStore
    ]

    Supervisor.init(children, strategy:
:one_for_all)
  end
end
```

Notice the strategy change: `:one_for_all` means that if any cache-related process dies, all related processes are restarted. This can be useful when you want to maintain consistency between cached items.

Organizing your processes this way makes it easier to understand, test, and monitor your application.

Supervision Strategies

Each Supervisor uses a **strategy** to determine how to handle child process failures:

`:one_for_one`: If a child crashes, only that child is restarted. This is the default and most common.

`:one_for_all`: If a child crashes, all siblings are terminated and restarted. Useful when processes are tightly coupled.

`:rest_for_one`: If a child crashes, the crashed process and all processes started **after it** are restarted. Useful when order matters (e.g., a process that depends on another).

Choosing the right strategy helps keep your system stable under partial failure.

Application Shutdown

When you shut down an Elixir application (using `System.stop/0`, `init.d`, `systemd`, or a node crash), the BEAM triggers a shutdown sequence:

Your top-level Supervisor receives an exit signal.

It sends `:shutdown` signals to all its children.

Each process can respond to `terminate/2` callbacks if needed.

Processes are given a window of time to clean up and shut down gracefully.

Finally, the VM exits.

If you have cleanup work (like closing database connections or writing final log entries), you can implement `terminate/2` inside your GenServer or Worker:

```
@impl true
def terminate(_reason, _state) do
  Logger.info("Cleaning up...")
  :ok
end
```

Elixir's focus on graceful shutdown ensures that even during crashes or redeployments, your system leaves minimal damage behind.

Real-World Example: Phoenix Application Boot

When you start a Phoenix application like this:

`MIX_ENV=prod mix phx.server`

This triggers:

Loading your compiled modules

Starting `MyApp.Application`

Launching your `Repo` (database connection pool)

Launching your `Endpoint` (HTTP server)

Starting background job processors (like Oban)

Starting internal caches or PubSub systems

Every piece is connected through a unified, supervised structure that can self-heal during partial failures and shut down cleanly when needed.

This architecture is why Phoenix apps can achieve incredible uptime even under network glitches, server maintenance, and user load spikes.

The structure and lifecycle of an Elixir application are not random—they are intentional, disciplined, and designed for fault tolerance. By understanding the Application module, supervision trees, strategies, startup sequence, and shutdown behavior, you can build systems that are:

Easier to reason about

More robust under failure

Naturally scalable as complexity grows

Maintainable and operationally safe in production

In the next section, we'll move into **designing resilient systems**—applying supervision principles to build self-healing, distributed architectures that stay responsive and correct even when parts of the system fail unpredictably.

Designing Resilient Systems

Resilience is not about preventing all failures. It's about **accepting that failures will happen** and designing your system to **recover quickly, safely, and predictably** without human intervention. In the Elixir ecosystem, resilience is a fundamental property, not an optional feature. Using the principles provided by OTP—especially processes, supervisors, and fault tolerance patterns—you can build applications that survive hardware failures, software bugs, and unpredictable external conditions.

In Elixir, processes are designed to **fail independently**. If a process crashes, it does not bring down other unrelated processes. This isolation is key to resilience.

Each GenServer you create, each Task you spawn, each supervised process— these are like little sandboxes. If one sandbox catches fire, it burns alone; it does not destroy the whole building.

Because of this, you should avoid building "monolith processes" that do too much. Instead:

Break your application into many small, isolated processes.

Give each process a focused responsibility.

Allow failures to be local instead of systemic.

Example: if you have 1,000 users connected to your Phoenix application through channels, each user's socket process is isolated. If one user's process crashes, the others continue uninterrupted.

Supervisors Make Recovery Automatic

A **Supervisor** in Elixir is responsible for watching child processes and restarting them according to a strategy.

Choosing the right supervision strategy improves your system's resilience:

:one_for_one: Restart only the crashed process. Best when processes are independent.

:one_for_all: Restart all processes if any one crashes. Useful when processes share state tightly (for example, a cache and a session handler tied together).

:rest_for_one: Restart the crashed process and all children started after it. Useful when initialization order matters (e.g., a manager and workers it spawned).

You define supervisors in a way that mirrors logical boundaries of your application.

Example:

```
defmodule MyApp.Supervisor do
  use Supervisor

  @impl true
  def start_link(_opts) do
    Supervisor.start_link(__MODULE__, :ok, name:
__MODULE__)
  end

  @impl true
  def init(:ok) do
    children = [
      MyApp.Repo,
      MyAppWeb.Endpoint,
      MyApp.CacheSupervisor,
      MyApp.BackgroundJobsSupervisor
    ]

    Supervisor.init(children, strategy:
:one_for_one)
  end
end
```

Each part of your system—web endpoints, caches, background job processors—is managed separately under the top-level supervisor. Failures are contained and recovered independently.

Fail Fast, Recover Fast

In resilient systems, it's better to **crash early** than to continue in a corrupted state.

Example:

```
@impl true
def handle_call({:get, key}, _from, nil) do
  raise "Unexpected nil state!"
end
```

If the internal state is invalid, raise an error and crash. Don't try to guess or silently continue. Silent errors accumulate and make the system unpredictable.

When your GenServer crashes:

The Supervisor sees the crash.

It restarts the GenServer immediately.

The new GenServer starts with a clean initial state.

Because processes are lightweight and supervisors are efficient, this crash-restart cycle can happen thousands of times per second without affecting the overall system stability.

This philosophy is often called **let it crash**. It's not about giving up—it's about trusting the supervision strategy to handle recovery faster and safer than complex defensive code would.

Isolate Critical Dependencies

External services (like APIs, databases, payment gateways) are common points of failure. You should isolate interactions with them into dedicated supervised processes.

Example:

```
defmodule MyApp.PaymentGateway do
  use GenServer

  def start_link(_args), do:
GenServer.start_link(__MODULE__, :ok, name:
__MODULE__)

  @impl true
  def init(:ok), do: {:ok, %{}}

  def charge(card_details) do
```

```
    GenServer.call(__MODULE__, {:charge,
card_details})
  end

  @impl true
  def handle_call({:charge, card_details}, _from,
state) do
    case ExternalAPI.charge(card_details) do
      {:ok, receipt} -> {:reply, {:ok, receipt},
state}
      {:error, reason} -> {:stop, {:shutdown,
reason}, state}
    end
  end
end
```

If the external API fails or behaves unexpectedly, the `PaymentGateway` GenServer can crash cleanly without corrupting the rest of your application. The supervisor restarts it automatically, and other parts of your system continue working.

You can combine this with **circuit breakers** (using libraries like `fuse`) to temporarily block calls to an unhealthy service.

Design Processes to Be Restart-Friendly

When a process restarts, it starts fresh. Therefore:

Don't store critical long-term data only in memory.

Persist important information in durable stores like PostgreSQL, Redis, or ETS tables managed separately.

Use external persistent systems for session state, queue management, and business-critical workflows.

Good design accepts that processes are temporary.

Example of statelessness-friendly design:

```
def handle_call(:get_order_status, _from, state) do
  {:reply,
Orders.fetch_status_from_db(state.order_id), state}
end
```

Instead of keeping order status in memory indefinitely, the GenServer fetches it fresh from a database when needed.

Monitoring and Observability

Resilient systems are observable systems. You should:

Emit Telemetry events from critical parts of your code.

Monitor crash rates, restart counts, queue sizes, and memory usage.

Use tools like Prometheus, Grafana, Sentry, or AppSignal to get live visibility into failures and recovery.

Example Telemetry instrumentation:

```
:telemetry.execute(

  [:my_app, :worker, :job_finished],

  %{duration: 12345},

  %{worker: "ReportGenerator"}

)
```

Monitoring helps you catch patterns of instability early, long before they escalate into user-facing issues.

Real-World Example: Resilient Chat Application

Suppose you are building a chat system.

Each room is a GenServer managing:

Connected users

Recent messages

Typing indicators

You supervise each room separately:

```
defmodule MyApp.Chat.RoomSupervisor do
  use DynamicSupervisor
```

```elixir
  def start_link(_opts), do:
DynamicSupervisor.start_link(__MODULE__, :ok, name:
  __MODULE__)

  @impl true
  def init(:ok) do
    DynamicSupervisor.init(strategy: :one_for_one)
  end

  def start_room(room_id) do
    child_spec = {MyApp.Chat.Room, room_id}
    DynamicSupervisor.start_child(__MODULE__,
child_spec)
  end
end
```

If a room process crashes (e.g., bad message encoding, heavy load), only that room restarts. Other rooms are unaffected. Users in the crashed room reconnect transparently. This keeps your system fast and responsive under partial failures.

Designing resilient systems in Elixir means trusting processes, supervisors, and the BEAM's failure handling capabilities. To achieve true resilience:

Design processes to fail fast and restart cleanly.

Organize supervision trees logically and thoughtfully.

Persist important data outside volatile processes.

Monitor the health of your system continuously.

Accept failure as a normal and manageable event.

In the next section, we'll bring all these concepts together with **practical OTP applications**—building real-world examples of how you can apply GenServers, Supervisors, and fault-tolerant design patterns to build production-grade systems that never stop serving your users.

Practical OTP Applications

Theory is important, but mastery comes when you see concepts applied to real problems. OTP isn't just an academic model—it's how production-grade systems are built and maintained. Whether you're building a live chat app, managing distributed background jobs, or coordinating a real-time leaderboard, OTP behaviors like **GenServer**, **Supervisor**, and **DynamicSupervisor** give you the building blocks to do it with reliability, clarity, and efficiency.

Building a Dynamic Chat Room Manager

Suppose you're tasked with creating a real-time chat system where users can create and join chat rooms dynamically. Each room should be isolated, and if a room crashes or becomes idle, it should recover or terminate cleanly.

First, define a Room process using GenServer:

```
defmodule MyApp.Chat.Room do
  use GenServer

  # Client API
  def start_link(room_id) do
    GenServer.start_link(__MODULE__, %{room_id:
room_id, users: []}, name: via_tuple(room_id))
  end

  def join(room_id, user_id) do
    GenServer.cast(via_tuple(room_id), {:join,
user_id})
  end

  def leave(room_id, user_id) do
    GenServer.cast(via_tuple(room_id), {:leave,
user_id})
  end

  defp via_tuple(room_id) do
    {:via, Registry, {MyApp.Chat.RoomRegistry,
room_id}}
  end

  # Server Callbacks
  @impl true
  def init(state), do: {:ok, state}
```

```elixir
  @impl true
  def handle_cast({:join, user_id}, state) do
    {:noreply, %{state | users: [user_id |
state.users]}}
  end

  @impl true
  def handle_cast({:leave, user_id}, state) do
    updated_users = List.delete(state.users,
user_id)

    if updated_users == [] do
      {:stop, :normal, %{state | users: []}}
    else
      {:noreply, %{state | users: updated_users}}
    end
  end
end
```

Each room is responsible for managing its own list of users. If the room becomes empty, it shuts down cleanly.

Next, manage dynamic room creation with a DynamicSupervisor:

```elixir
defmodule MyApp.Chat.RoomSupervisor do
  use DynamicSupervisor

  def start_link(_opts) do
    DynamicSupervisor.start_link(__MODULE__, :ok,
name: __MODULE__)
  end

  @impl true
  def init(:ok), do:
DynamicSupervisor.init(strategy: :one_for_one)

  def start_room(room_id) do
    child_spec = {MyApp.Chat.Room, room_id}
    DynamicSupervisor.start_child(__MODULE__,
child_spec)
  end
end
```

Use a Registry to map room IDs to processes:

```elixir
defmodule MyApp.Chat.RoomRegistry do

  use Registry,

    keys: :unique,

    name: MyApp.Chat.RoomRegistry

end
```

Startup configuration:

```elixir
children = [
  {Registry, keys: :unique, name:
MyApp.Chat.RoomRegistry},
  MyApp.Chat.RoomSupervisor
]
```

When a user creates or joins a room:

```elixir
# Create the room if it doesn't exist
MyApp.Chat.RoomSupervisor.start_room("sports")

# User joins
MyApp.Chat.Room.join("sports", "user_123")
```

Now each chat room:

Is a supervised, isolated GenServer.

Manages its own state independently.

Shuts down cleanly when empty.

Can be recreated dynamically at any time.

This design is clean, scalable, and matches real production needs without external dependencies.

Building a Real-Time Leaderboard

A leaderboard system where scores are updated rapidly and rankings are recalculated frequently requires fast reads and writes without relying heavily on a database.

You can build it in OTP using ETS (Erlang Term Storage) combined with a GenServer.

Define the Leaderboard Server:

```
defmodule MyApp.Leaderboard do
  use GenServer

  @table :leaderboard_scores

  def start_link(_opts) do
    GenServer.start_link(__MODULE__, %{}, name:
__MODULE__)
  end

  # Client API
  def submit_score(player_id, score) do
    GenServer.cast(__MODULE__, {:submit_score,
player_id, score})
  end

  def top_n(n) do
    :ets.tab2list(@table)
    |> Enum.sort_by(fn {_player_id, score} -> -
score end)
    |> Enum.take(n)
  end

  # Server Callbacks
  @impl true
  def init(_state) do
    :ets.new(@table, [:named_table, :public,
read_concurrency: true])
    {:ok, %{}}
  end

  @impl true
  def handle_cast({:submit_score, player_id,
score}, state) do
```

```
    :ets.insert(@table, {player_id, score})
    {:noreply, state}
  end
end
```

Using ETS allows you to read scores without needing to send a message to the GenServer, enabling thousands of reads per second with minimal latency.

Use it like:

```
MyApp.Leaderboard.submit_score("player_1", 1200)
MyApp.Leaderboard.submit_score("player_2", 1400)

MyApp.Leaderboard.top_n(5)
# => [{"player_2", 1400}, {"player_1", 1200}]
```

This model ensures:

Updates are serialized through the GenServer (to prevent race conditions).

Reads are fast and concurrent thanks to ETS.

The Leaderboard process is supervised and can recover if it crashes by simply resetting the scores.

Background Data Synchronization

Sometimes you need to sync data from an external API at regular intervals. Instead of relying on external cron jobs or manual triggers, you can create a GenServer with a timer.

Example:

```
defmodule MyApp.DataSync do
  use GenServer

  @sync_interval :timer.minutes(10)

  def start_link(_opts), do:
GenServer.start_link(__MODULE__, :ok, name:
  __MODULE__)

  @impl true
  def init(:ok) do
```

```
    schedule_sync()
    {:ok, %{}}
  end

  @impl true
  def handle_info(:sync, state) do
    fetch_and_update_data()
    schedule_sync()
    {:noreply, state}
  end

  defp schedule_sync do
    Process.send_after(self(), :sync,
@sync_interval)
  end

  defp fetch_and_update_data do
    case ExternalAPI.fetch_data() do
      {:ok, data} -> MyApp.DataStore.update(data)
      {:error, reason} -> Logger.error("Failed to
sync: #{inspect(reason)}")
    end
  end
end
```

Now, every 10 minutes, your app pulls the latest data automatically, recovers from temporary failures, and logs errors if the API is unreachable.

This is efficient, reliable, and fits cleanly into the OTP supervision system.

Best Practices for Practical OTP Applications

Keep your GenServers small, focused, and restartable.

Use DynamicSupervisors when you need processes that can come and go.

Use ETS for read-heavy, volatile data where high concurrency is needed.

Persist critical long-term state (like user accounts or orders) in durable databases.

Monitor and log errors clearly to spot issues early.

Let processes crash when they hit unrecoverable errors instead of trying to patch broken state.

By applying OTP patterns correctly, you can build:

Scalable chat systems

Fast and concurrent leaderboards

Reliable background data synchronizers

Fault-tolerant, self-healing distributed systems

These are not theoretical skills—they are real capabilities that you can use today to build production systems that handle millions of users, recover from partial failures automatically, and require minimal manual maintenance.

Chapter 9: Scaling Phoenix Applications

Building an application that works well in development is one thing. Scaling it to support thousands or millions of users across multiple machines is another. Fortunately, Phoenix applications—backed by the Elixir runtime and the BEAM—are built with concurrency, distribution, and fault-tolerance in mind from the start. But that doesn't mean everything scales automatically. You still need to make the right architectural decisions, particularly when it comes to clustering, messaging, and shared state.

In this chapter, we'll focus on **practical strategies for scaling Phoenix applications**, with special attention to clustering with `libcluster`, using distributed PubSub and Presence, and managing state in multi-node deployments. These aren't abstract concepts—they're the foundations of building high-availability systems that stay responsive, consistent, and fault-tolerant as they grow.

Strategies for Scaling Elixir Systems

Elixir and the BEAM virtual machine were designed from the beginning to run highly available, fault-tolerant systems. However, as your application grows—from serving a handful of users in development to supporting tens of thousands or more in production—you must apply deliberate scaling strategies. Scaling is not automatic; it depends on how you structure processes, manage state, use hardware, and design distributed behavior.

Vertical Scaling: Getting the Most From a Single Node

Before you move to a distributed cluster, it's often smart to push a single node as far as it can reasonably go. Elixir applications can achieve impressive concurrency levels on a powerful server because each BEAM process is extremely lightweight.

A few steps to maximize a single node's performance:

Tune the number of schedulers: By default, the BEAM sets the number of schedulers to the number of CPU cores. You can control this explicitly:

```
ERL_FLAGS="+S 32:32" mix phx.server
```

This configures 32 scheduler threads, appropriate for a machine with 32 CPU cores.

Use process-based concurrency: Instead of long-running blocking operations, design the system to spawn processes liberally. Thousands of lightweight processes can run simultaneously without contention.

Offload slow tasks: Move slow tasks such as file processing, API calls, and email sending into background jobs (using Oban or Task.Supervisor) rather than blocking the main request/response cycle.

Reduce process mailbox bloat: Monitor process mailboxes. If processes build up unprocessed messages, they can become overloaded and cause cascading delays. Use Telemetry and metrics dashboards to track mailbox sizes if needed.

Example:

Suppose you're handling thousands of chat messages per second. Instead of processing each message serially, you can process each one in an isolated Task:

```
def handle_in("new_message", payload, socket) do
  Task.start(fn ->
MyApp.Chat.process_message(payload) end)
  {:noreply, socket}
end
```

The BEAM efficiently schedules thousands of these without starving other processes.

Vertical scaling works well until you saturate CPU or memory. Then, it's time to think about horizontal scaling.

Horizontal Scaling: Distributing the Load Across Nodes

When a single node can no longer handle the load, or you need better availability, you scale horizontally by running multiple instances of your application.

Key points in horizontal scaling:

Clustering: Connect your nodes together so they can communicate internally. This enables distributed features like PubSub, Presence, and global process registries.

Stateless web layer: Design your HTTP endpoints so that no state is stored in memory between requests. Database sessions, authentication tokens, and caches should be shared or externalized.

Load balancing: Use an external load balancer (like NGINX, HAProxy, AWS ALB) to distribute traffic among your nodes.

Sticky sessions (when needed): If you use WebSockets or LiveView heavily, you may need sticky sessions so that a client stays connected to the same node after initial handshake. Not strictly required if you use distributed PubSub correctly, but it simplifies state management.

Example architecture with horizontal scaling:

3 Phoenix application nodes

1 Redis server for distributed PubSub and Presence synchronization

PostgreSQL database for persistent storage

Load balancer distributing HTTP and WebSocket traffic

Each node is a complete application instance, capable of handling both real-time and request/response traffic. If a node fails, others continue serving users.

Minimizing State for Better Scalability

The less critical state you keep in memory per node, the easier it is to scale horizontally.

Bad design:

Keeping active cart data or user preferences only in GenServer state on a single node.

Good design:

Persisting carts and preferences in PostgreSQL or ETS-backed caches synchronized with the database.

Using Phoenix Presence for real-time ephemeral state like "user is online" indicators.

When you design state this way:

Crashes don't lose important data.

New nodes can serve users immediately without needing session synchronization.

Example:

Instead of managing an in-memory list of active users in a GenServer, you use Phoenix Presence, which broadcasts diffs to all nodes.

Room channel setup:

```
def join("room:" <> room_id, _params, socket) do
  send(self(), :after_join)
  {:ok, socket}
end

def handle_info(:after_join, socket) do
  MyApp.Presence.track(socket,
"room:#{socket.assigns.room_id}",
socket.assigns.user_id, %{})
  push(socket, "presence_state",
MyApp.Presence.list("room:#{socket.assigns.room_id}
"))
  {:noreply, socket}
end
```

Now, user presence is consistent across nodes without manual intervention.

Monitoring and Load Testing

Scaling without measuring is blind guessing. You must observe your system under load to know where bottlenecks form.

Good practices:

Use :telemetry events to capture request durations, database query times, and process counts.

Visualize data with Prometheus + Grafana or tools like Datadog, AppSignal, or Sentry.

Use `wrk`, `k6`, or `Gatling` for realistic load testing before going live.

Simple Telemetry example:

```
:telemetry.execute([:my_app, :endpoint, :stop],
%{duration: 1_234_567}, %{path: "/api/posts"})
```

Then you can graph latency distributions, error rates, and throughput easily.

Early detection allows you to tune your cluster size, queue workers, and database performance before problems hit users.

Real-World Scaling Example: Live Auctions

Suppose you're building a live auction platform where thousands of users can watch bids update in real time.

Scaling considerations:

Each auction has its own channel topic.

PubSub broadcasts updates across nodes.

Presence tracks active bidders per auction.

Redis backs PubSub for multi-node broadcast.

libcluster ensures nodes discover each other dynamically.

Setup:

Kubernetes deploys 10 nodes, automatically scaling up under load.

PostgreSQL holds bids, auction states, and user registrations.

Oban workers handle post-auction processing asynchronously.

This design allows you to handle massive bid activity bursts while maintaining low latencies across globally distributed users.

Scaling Elixir systems is about aligning your application architecture with the capabilities of the BEAM:

Maximize concurrency and lightweight process usage on a single node first.

Distribute horizontally with libcluster, distributed PubSub, and external durable storage.

Minimize long-lived in-memory state; externalize important data.

Monitor everything, and load-test realistically.

Embrace dynamic, supervised, self-healing process structures.

With these strategies, you can confidently build systems that are fast, resilient, and ready to grow without re-architecting every time traffic increases.

Clustering with libcluster

In a distributed Elixir system, clustering is how multiple nodes discover each other, connect, and start communicating seamlessly as if they were part of a single unified system. Clustering allows processes on different nodes to send messages to each other, replicate data, synchronize PubSub events, share presence information, and recover from node failures without downtime.

Setting up clustering manually is tedious and error-prone. That's why `libcluster` exists. It automates node discovery, connection management, and ensures your cluster remains healthy—even as nodes dynamically come online or go offline.

At its core, `libcluster` monitors a source of truth (DNS, Kubernetes API, static IP list, etc.) to find other nodes that should join the cluster.

When a new node is detected:

libcluster tells the local node to connect using Erlang's built-in `:net_kernel.connect_node/1`.

Once connected, both nodes become part of a distributed system.

Processes can communicate freely across nodes using just process identifiers (PIDs) or registered names.

When a node disappears:

libcluster notices the absence.

If necessary, systems relying on node presence (like distributed registries) can clean up resources automatically.

It keeps your cluster healthy **without manual intervention**.

Installing libcluster

First, add libcluster to your project's dependencies:

```
# mix.exs
defp deps do
    [
        {:libcluster, "~> 3.3"}
    ]
end
```

Fetch the dependencies:

```
mix deps.get
```

You are now ready to configure clustering.

Configuring libcluster

How you configure libcluster depends on where you are running your application.

Static configuration for local development

Suppose you're running two nodes on your local machine and want them to connect manually.

In `config/config.exs`:

```
config :libcluster,
   topologies: [
     example: [
        strategy: Cluster.Strategy.Epmd,
        config: [
          hosts: [:"node1@127.0.0.1",
:"node2@127.0.0.1"]
        ]
     ]
   ]
```

Here, `hosts` lists the nodes explicitly.

You can start nodes like:

```
iex --sname node1 -S mix phx.server

iex --sname node2 -S mix phx.server
```

Both nodes will automatically connect.

Dynamic configuration for Kubernetes

For production, you don't want hardcoded IPs. Instead, use Kubernetes DNS discovery.

Example for Kubernetes:

```
config :libcluster,
  topologies: [
    k8s_example: [
      strategy: Cluster.Strategy.Kubernetes.DNS,
      config: [
        service: "myapp-headless",
        application_name: "my_app",
        polling_interval: 5_000
      ]
    ]
  ]
```

Here:

`service` is the name of your Kubernetes **headless** service.

`application_name` is used for filtering pods.

`polling_interval` controls how often it checks for new nodes.

You must also create a headless service:

```
apiVersion: v1
kind: Service
metadata:
  name: myapp-headless
spec:
  clusterIP: None
```

```
selector:
    app: myapp
  ports:
  - port: 4000
    targetPort: 4000
```

This service enables DNS records like `myapp-headless.default.svc.cluster.local`, listing all pod IPs.

Adding libcluster to Your Supervision Tree

After configuring, you must start libcluster's supervisor inside your application.

In `application.ex`:

```
def start(_type, _args) do
  children = [
    {Cluster.Supervisor,
[Application.get_env(:libcluster, :topologies),
[name: MyApp.ClusterSupervisor]]},
    MyApp.Repo,
    MyAppWeb.Endpoint
  ]

  opts = [strategy: :one_for_one, name:
MyApp.Supervisor]
  Supervisor.start_link(children, opts)
end
```

Now, when your app boots, it automatically starts discovering and connecting to peer nodes.

You can verify connections by running in IEx:

```
Node.list()
```

It should show connected nodes.

Working With Clusters: Practical Patterns

Once your nodes are connected, they behave like one big system.

Common practical patterns:

Distributed PubSub: Set up PubSub with a distributed backend (Redis or PostgreSQL) so broadcasts reach all nodes.

Presence Tracking: Track users across nodes without worrying about manual syncs.

Distributed GenServers: Use libraries like Horde or Swarm if you need one GenServer per resource globally across nodes.

Job Distribution: Tools like Oban Pro's Queues feature allow distributed job execution across cluster nodes.

Example: **distributed presence tracking**

You can track users across a cluster using Phoenix Presence:

```
defmodule MyAppWeb.Presence do

  use Phoenix.Presence,

    otp_app: :my_app,

    pubsub_server: MyApp.PubSub

end
```

Each node updates Presence locally, and diff updates are broadcast across the cluster via PubSub.

Clients connected to different nodes all see consistent user counts and statuses without knowing about clustering at all.

Handling Network Partitions

One reality of distributed systems is that nodes can temporarily lose connectivity (called a partition or "net split").

Elixir nodes try to heal automatically, but some strategies help:

Use CRDTs (Conflict-Free Replicated Data Types) for Presence so merges are safe.

Favor **eventual consistency** models over strong immediate consistency.

Monitor node connectivity with `:net_kernel.monitor_nodes/1` if you want to detect partitions manually:

```
:net_kernel.monitor_nodes(true)
```

Now your process will receive `{:nodeup, node}` and `{:nodedown, node}` messages you can react to.

Example:

```
def handle_info({:nodedown, node}, state) do

  Logger.warn("Lost connection to #{inspect(node)}")

  {:noreply, state}

end
```

This lets you implement custom handling logic like redistributing workloads.

Real-World Example: A Global Live Game

Suppose you build a live trivia game platform.

Each question round is a topic ("round:123").

Players are connected to different nodes.

Game state (questions, timers) must synchronize instantly.

You deploy across multiple data centers.

Setup:

libcluster handles automatic node discovery.

Phoenix PubSub distributes broadcast messages to all nodes.

Redis backs PubSub across regions.

Presence tracks active players across topics.

When a new question appears, the master process broadcasts:

```
MyAppWeb.Endpoint.broadcast!("round:123",
"new_question", %{question: "What is 2+2?"})
```

Every player, no matter which server they are connected to, receives the update at the same moment.

Failures of a node only affect players connected to that specific node, and reconnect logic can restore them to the game instantly.

libcluster is a critical tool that makes clustering Elixir nodes effortless and robust:

It automatically discovers and connects nodes at runtime.

It integrates cleanly with Phoenix PubSub and Presence.

It enables building real distributed applications without massive code changes.

It supports multiple discovery strategies like static lists, DNS, Kubernetes, and cloud APIs.

With libcluster set up properly, your Phoenix or Elixir application can scale horizontally, stay resilient under load, and deliver seamless real-time features to users, even in the face of node failures and dynamic scaling events.

Distributed PubSub and Presence

When you build real-time features like chat systems, notifications, or collaborative editing tools, you need a way for different parts of your system to broadcast messages and track connected users. In a simple single-node Phoenix application, this is easy: everything is local, and processes share memory naturally. But once you scale your application across multiple nodes—whether across different machines, containers, or datacenters—you must ensure that broadcasting and user tracking remain consistent and seamless.

This is where **Phoenix PubSub** and **Phoenix Presence** shine. Together, they provide the tools you need to send messages across your entire distributed cluster and track user sessions reliably—even when users are connected to different servers.

PubSub stands for **Publish-Subscribe**. It is a messaging pattern where:

A process **publishes** an event to a topic.

Other processes **subscribed** to that topic receive the event.

Phoenix PubSub makes this very easy. When your application is running on a single node, PubSub uses ETS tables and internal messaging to handle everything. But when you have multiple nodes, you must distribute the messages across all nodes.

Phoenix PubSub supports different backends for this:

Local (default for single node)

Redis

PostgreSQL

Distributed Erlang (for clustered nodes without an external system)

The choice of backend depends on your deployment environment. Redis is the most common because it's simple and reliable.

Configuring Distributed PubSub with Redis

First, add the required dependency:

```
# mix.exs

defp deps do

    [

      {:phoenix_pubsub_redis, "~> 3.0"}

    ]

end
```

Fetch the dependency:

```
mix deps.get
```

Then configure PubSub to use Redis in your `config.exs`:

```
config :my_app, MyApp.PubSub,
```

```
adapter: Phoenix.PubSub.Redis,

url: "redis://localhost:6379"
```

Make sure your Phoenix Endpoint is using your PubSub server:

```
# endpoint.ex

pubsub_server: MyApp.PubSub
```

Now, when you call:

```
MyAppWeb.Endpoint.broadcast!("topic:123",
"new_message", %{content: "Hello"})
```

Phoenix will:

Send the message to the local subscribers.

Publish it to Redis.

Other nodes will receive the message from Redis and dispatch it to their local subscribers.

This keeps all nodes synchronized without needing direct node-to-node connections.

Broadcasting and Subscribing in Practice

Subscribing to a topic:

```
Phoenix.PubSub.subscribe(MyApp.PubSub, "topic:123")
```

Broadcasting a message:

```
Phoenix.PubSub.broadcast(MyApp.PubSub, "topic:123",
%{event: "new_message", payload: %{text: "Hi
there"}})
```

Or through the Endpoint helper:

```
MyAppWeb.Endpoint.broadcast!("topic:123",
"new_message", %{text: "Hi there"})
```

On the receiving end, the subscribed process will receive:

```
%Phoenix.Socket.Broadcast{event: "new_message",
payload: %{text: "Hi there"}, topic: "topic:123"}
```

This design allows **channels, LiveViews,** or any process to stay in sync across a large distributed cluster without worrying about where users are connected.

Understanding Phoenix Presence

PubSub handles messaging. **Presence** handles **who** is connected and **where**.

Presence lets you:

Track connected users per topic.

Track metadata (like username, online status, current page).

Automatically synchronize joins and leaves across all nodes.

Presence uses **CRDTs** (Conflict-Free Replicated Data Types) under the hood. This means even if the network splits temporarily, the nodes will eventually converge to the same consistent state without manual intervention.

Setting Up Presence

Define a Presence module:

```
defmodule MyAppWeb.Presence do

  use Phoenix.Presence,

    otp_app: :my_app,

    pubsub_server: MyApp.PubSub

end
```
Track a user when they join a channel:

```
def handle_info(:after_join, socket) do
  MyAppWeb.Presence.track(
    socket,
    socket.assigns.user_id,
    %{
      online_at: System.system_time(:second),
      page: "dashboard"
    }
```

```
  )

  push(socket, "presence_state",
MyAppWeb.Presence.list(socket))
  {:noreply, socket}
end
```

`track/3` registers the user with optional metadata.

`list/1` shows all currently tracked users in the topic.

When users join or leave, Presence automatically broadcasts diffs to all subscribers, even across nodes.

Example: Real-Time Collaborative Document Editing

Suppose you're building a collaborative document editor. Each document is a topic like `"doc:456"`.

When users open the document, they join `"doc:456"`.

You track each user with Presence, including their cursor position.

Changes are broadcast using PubSub to all users subscribed to that topic.

Joining a document channel:

```
def join("doc:" <> _doc_id, _params, socket) do

  send(self(), :after_join)

  {:ok, socket}

end
```

After joining:

```
def handle_info(:after_join, socket) do
  MyAppWeb.Presence.track(
    socket,
    socket.assigns.user_id,
    %{cursor: %{line: 1, column: 1}}
  )
```

```
  push(socket, "presence_state",
MyAppWeb.Presence.list(socket))
  {:noreply, socket}
end
```

Now everyone editing the same document, even across different servers, sees each other's presence and cursor movements live.

When a user moves their cursor:

```
broadcast_from(socket, "cursor_moved", %{line: 5, column: 10})
```

Other users update their UI instantly, regardless of which server they're connected to.

Important Considerations for PubSub and Presence

Use **meaningful topic names** to partition traffic efficiently (e.g., one topic per room, document, or group).

Be aware that **broadcasting** large payloads frequently can add significant load—keep payloads minimal.

Presence metadata should be small and updated only when necessary (for example, when a user switches pages or moves their cursor).

Redis PubSub doesn't guarantee **persistence**. If a node is down when a message is broadcast, it will miss that event. Design your system to tolerate occasional missed ephemeral updates if necessary.

For critical guaranteed delivery, consider coupling with persistent job systems or event stores.

Distributed PubSub and Presence are essential tools for building scalable real-time Elixir applications:

PubSub enables broadcasting messages across multiple nodes seamlessly.

Presence tracks users across topics and nodes, keeping real-time metadata synchronized automatically.

Together, they support building real-time chat apps, collaborative editors, multiplayer games, and notification systems at scale.

With PubSub and Presence properly configured, your Phoenix application can support live features across a distributed cluster without extra complexity, keeping users engaged and synchronized no matter where they connect from.

Managing State Across Nodes

When your Elixir application grows beyond a single server, managing state correctly becomes one of the most critical challenges. In a single-node system, holding process state in memory is often safe and efficient. But in a distributed cluster, processes might crash, nodes might disappear, network partitions might occur, and yet your application still needs to remain functional, consistent, and resilient.

Managing state across nodes requires thoughtful strategies: deciding **what kind of state** you're dealing with, **where it should live**, and **how it should recover** when things go wrong.

Different Types of State and How They Behave Across Nodes

Not all state is the same. Managing it correctly depends on what kind of state you're handling.

Ephemeral state: Temporary, non-critical information (e.g., who is currently typing, a temporary session token). If lost, it's annoying but not catastrophic.
Managed best with **Presence**, **local processes**, or **temporary ETS tables**.

Persistent business state: Critical information (e.g., user accounts, invoices, shopping carts) that must never be lost.
Managed through **databases** like PostgreSQL.

Process state: In-memory state held by a GenServer. Often fast and convenient, but **volatile**.
Managed using supervised processes, and when needed, recovered from durable sources.

Global coordination state: Shared state across all nodes, such as cluster-wide registries or global counters.
Managed using tools like **Horde**, **Swarm**, or **Mnesia** (with careful consideration).

Best Practices for Managing State in a Distributed Elixir Application

1. Store Critical Data Outside of Processes

Processes are not durable. If a GenServer holding your shopping cart state crashes, the cart disappears unless you persist it elsewhere.

Always store business-critical data in an external system like:

PostgreSQL

Redis (for semi-persistent caching)

Mnesia (only for very specific use cases)

Example:

Instead of keeping an in-memory list of orders:

```
def handle_call(:list_orders, _from, orders), do:
{:reply, orders, orders}
```

You should persist orders in the database and fetch them when needed:

```
def handle_call(:list_orders, _from, _state) do
  orders = MyApp.Orders.list_all()
  {:reply, orders, %{}}
end
```

This ensures that even if the GenServer or node crashes, your data is safe.

2. Use Phoenix Presence for Ephemeral State

Presence is ideal for managing volatile, per-session state like:

"User is online"

"User is typing"

"User is viewing page X"

Presence uses CRDTs under the hood, meaning updates merge cleanly even across network partitions.

When a user connects to a channel:

```
MyAppWeb.Presence.track(
```

```
  socket,
  socket.assigns.user_id,
  %{online_at: System.system_time(:second)}
)
```

When they disconnect, Presence cleans up automatically.

Presence state is resilient but ephemeral. If a node goes down, you might temporarily lose presence information, but the system self-heals.

3. Partition State Across Nodes When Possible

Not every process needs to know everything.

Example: a chat system with 10,000 rooms.

Rather than one GenServer holding all rooms, use a DynamicSupervisor where each room is a separate process:

```
def start_link(room_id) do

  GenServer.start_link(__MODULE__, room_id, name:
via_tuple(room_id))

end



defp via_tuple(room_id), do: {:via, Registry,
{MyApp.RoomRegistry, room_id}}
```

Each node can host a portion of the rooms, balancing the load naturally across the cluster.

When using `Registry`, processes are local to the node. If a node crashes, the associated rooms are lost, but you can rebuild them from persistent data if needed.

4. When Global Processes Are Necessary, Use Horde or Swarm

Sometimes you need a **single global process** managing a resource, such as:

A user-specific real-time data feed

A leader election mechanism

Libraries like **Horde** help you manage distributed dynamic supervisors and registries.

Example:

```
defmodule MyApp.UserSupervisor do
  use Horde.DynamicSupervisor

  def start_link(opts) do
    Horde.DynamicSupervisor.start_link(__MODULE__,
opts, name: __MODULE__)
  end

  @impl true
  def init(_init_arg) do
    [strategy: :one_for_one, distribution_strategy:
Horde.UniformDistribution]
  end
end
```

With Horde, your supervisors are globally aware:

Processes are evenly distributed across the cluster.

If a node crashes, Horde automatically restarts orphaned processes on surviving nodes.

Registry state is synchronized automatically.

This greatly simplifies building globally resilient services.

5. Understand Eventual Consistency

In distributed systems, you must often accept **eventual consistency** instead of immediate consistency.

Example:

A user's Presence may not reflect their online status instantly after a network partition.

A dynamic room process may migrate to another node after a crash, and clients must reconnect.

Designing your app to tolerate slight inconsistencies temporarily leads to better availability and simpler code.

Use **broadcast and converge** patterns:

Broadcast updates optimistically.

Periodically resynchronize with a durable source if needed.

Real-World Example: Scalable Notification Service

Suppose you are building a notification system that delivers real-time alerts to users.

Design:

Each user has a personal topic: `"user:notifications:#{user_id}"`.

Notifications are stored persistently in PostgreSQL.

Live notifications are broadcast through Phoenix PubSub.

Presence tracks which users are online.

When sending a notification:

```
def send_notification(user_id, payload) do

MyAppWeb.Endpoint.broadcast!("user:notifications:#{
user_id}", "new_notification", payload)

  if not user_online?(user_id) do

MyApp.Notifications.persist_notification(user_id,
payload)
  end
end

defp user_online?(user_id) do

MyAppWeb.Presence.list("user:notifications:#{user_i
d}") != %{}
end
```

If the user is online, they receive it live. If not, the notification is saved for later retrieval.

Even if a node crash happens, no notification is lost.

Common Pitfalls to Avoid

Relying too much on process state: Always ask whether it's acceptable to lose the state if the node dies. If not, persist it elsewhere.

Expecting instant global consistency: In a real distributed system, it's better to design for eventual consistency and healing.

Building huge monolithic processes: Break your system into many small, isolated processes that supervisors can restart independently.

Managing state across nodes is not about eliminating failure—it's about **embracing and preparing for it**. In a distributed Elixir system:

Persist important business data externally.

Use Presence for ephemeral, session-bound tracking.

Partition and distribute state intelligently across nodes.

Use libraries like Horde for global process management when necessary.

Design for eventual consistency, not strict synchrony.

By following these principles, your Phoenix application will not only scale but remain resilient and responsive even as users, nodes, and network conditions change dynamically.

Chapter 10: Testing and Debugging Elixir and Phoenix Apps

Building scalable and distributed Phoenix applications is powerful, but no real system reaches production quality without serious attention to **testing** and **debugging**. A distributed, fault-tolerant architecture doesn't replace the need for careful validation—it demands it even more.

Testing in Elixir is not an afterthought. Thanks to tools like **ExUnit**, **Phoenix testing modules**, **StreamData**, and a strong ecosystem of observability tools, you can ensure your applications behave correctly even under unexpected conditions. And when things inevitably go wrong, Elixir's runtime and tooling give you the insights you need to diagnose and fix issues quickly.

Unit Testing with ExUnit

Unit testing is one of the strongest habits you can develop as an Elixir developer. It allows you to verify that each piece of your code behaves correctly in isolation. Elixir's standard testing framework, **ExUnit**, makes writing and running unit tests extremely straightforward. It's built into the language, requires no third-party libraries, and integrates smoothly with Elixir's tooling.

Setting Up ExUnit

You don't need to install anything separately. ExUnit is part of Elixir's standard library.

When you create a new Phoenix project or a pure Elixir project using `mix new`, ExUnit is already set up for you. You will find a `test` directory containing files like:

```
test/

  my_app_test.exs

  test_helper.exs
```

The `test_helper.exs` file calls `ExUnit.start()`, which boots the testing environment.

To run your tests:

```
mix test
```

ExUnit will automatically find all files ending in _test.exs under the test/ directory and run them.

Writing a Simple Test Case

Tests are written inside modules that use ExUnit.Case. Each test is a function defined with the test macro.

Here's a simple example:

```
defmodule MyApp.MathTest do
  use ExUnit.Case, async: true

  test "adds two numbers correctly" do
    assert MyApp.Math.add(1, 2) == 3
  end

  test "subtracts two numbers correctly" do
    assert MyApp.Math.subtract(5, 3) == 2
  end
end
```

Key points:

async: true allows tests in this module to run concurrently with tests in other modules. Use it when the tests don't interact with shared resources (like a database).

assert verifies that an expression evaluates to true.

If an assertion fails, the test fails and ExUnit reports it clearly.

You can group related tests in the same module and use meaningful descriptions to make failures easy to understand.

Common Assertions

ExUnit provides a set of built-in assertions that cover most typical testing needs:

```
assert value == expected_value

refute value == unexpected_value

assert_raise ErrorModule, fn ->
code_that_should_fail() end

assert_received message

assert_in_delta float1, float2, allowed_difference
```

Example: testing for an exception:

```
test "raises on invalid input" do
  assert_raise ArgumentError, fn ->
    MyApp.Math.divide(10, 0)
  end
end
```

This ensures that your code behaves correctly even when errors are supposed to happen.

Setting Up Common Test Data

You often need to prepare some state before running a test. ExUnit allows you to define setup blocks.

Example:

```
defmodule MyApp.AccountsTest do
  use ExUnit.Case

  setup do
    user = MyApp.AccountsFixtures.create_user()
    %{user: user}
  end

  test "retrieves a user by id", %{user: user} do
    found_user = MyApp.Accounts.get_user!(user.id)
    assert found_user.email == user.email
  end
end
```

Here:

`setup` runs before each test.

It returns a map that is injected into each test's context (`%{}`).

This keeps your tests clean and avoids repeated boilerplate.

If you need something to run once for all tests (for example, connecting to an external service), you can use `setup_all`.

Testing with Tags and Filters

ExUnit allows you to tag tests, making it easy to selectively run only a subset.

Example:

```
@tag :slow
test "complex calculation" do
  assert MyApp.Complex.calculate_heavy(5) == 42
end
```

Now you can run only fast tests:

```
mix test --exclude slow
```

Or run only slow tests:

```
mix test --only slow
```

This is helpful when your test suite grows large and you want quick feedback during development without running integration tests every time.

Testing Edge Cases and Invalid Inputs

Good unit tests don't just verify the "happy path." They also validate edge cases, bad data, and potential failure modes.

Example:

```
test "returns an error when user not found" do
  assert {:error, :not_found} =
MyApp.Accounts.get_user(-1)
end
```

By anticipating failure scenarios early, you make your code more defensive and your system more reliable in production.

Example: Testing a Simple Service Module

Let's say you have a simple service module:

```
defmodule MyApp.Greeter do
  def greet(nil), do: "Hello, Guest!"
  def greet(name), do: "Hello, #{name}!"
end
```

A corresponding test could be:

```
defmodule MyApp.GreeterTest do
  use ExUnit.Case, async: true

  test "greets a user by name" do
    assert MyApp.Greeter.greet("Nehemiah") ==
"Hello, Nehemiah!"
  end

  test "greets a guest when name is nil" do
    assert MyApp.Greeter.greet(nil) == "Hello,
Guest!"
  end
end
```

These tests are fast, deterministic, and give you confidence that your Greeter module behaves correctly.

Why Write Unit Tests?

Unit tests have several practical benefits:

Prevent regressions: When you change code, tests catch accidental breakage immediately.

Document behavior: Reading the tests often explains how the system should behave faster than reading the source code.

Speed up development: Safe refactoring becomes much easier when tests verify correctness automatically.

Catch edge cases early: Good tests force you to think about what can go wrong before users discover it.

Testing is not a burden. It is a professional tool that multiplies your productivity, confidence, and system quality.

ExUnit is a powerful, lightweight, and expressive testing framework that empowers you to:

Write clear, isolated unit tests.

Set up and tear down test resources cleanly.

Assert both expected behavior and proper error handling.

Tag and filter tests for focused runs.

Catch edge cases before they cause production incidents.

By embracing unit testing with ExUnit as a core part of your development workflow, you lay the foundation for building resilient, maintainable, and highly reliable Elixir and Phoenix applications.

Testing Controllers, Channels, and LiveViews

Testing individual functions is a great start, but modern Phoenix applications are made of more than just functions. Controllers handle HTTP requests, Channels manage real-time communication over WebSockets, and LiveViews create rich, reactive user interfaces without writing JavaScript. To ensure your system works as users expect, you need to test these components thoroughly.

Phoenix makes it straightforward to test controllers, channels, and LiveViews using specialized test modules. In this section, you'll learn how to write practical, comprehensive tests for each layer of your Phoenix application, ensuring everything from API endpoints to real-time updates behaves correctly.

Testing Controllers

Controllers handle incoming HTTP requests, often orchestrating business logic and rendering responses. In Phoenix, you can test them without running a real server using the **ConnCase** module.

ConnCase gives you a fresh `conn` struct in each test, simulating a request/response cycle cleanly and quickly.

Example: testing a simple controller

Suppose you have a controller:

```
defmodule MyAppWeb.PageController do
  use MyAppWeb, :controller

  def index(conn, _params) do
    text(conn, "Welcome to MyApp")
  end
end
```

You can test it like this:

```
defmodule MyAppWeb.PageControllerTest do
  use MyAppWeb.ConnCase, async: true

  test "GET / returns welcome text", %{conn: conn} do
    conn = get(conn, "/")
    assert text_response(conn, 200) == "Welcome to MyApp"
  end
end
```

`get/2` simulates a GET request to /.

`text_response/2` extracts the response body and asserts the HTTP status.

Testing JSON responses is just as easy:

```
test "GET /api/status returns JSON", %{conn: conn} do
  conn = get(conn, "/api/status")
  assert json_response(conn, 200) == %{"status" => "ok"}
end
```

Controller tests validate:

Routes are wired correctly.

Parameters are handled properly.

The right response (status, headers, body) is returned.

You can also simulate authenticated requests by manipulating the `conn` struct inside your setup block.

Testing Channels

Channels manage real-time WebSocket communication, and Phoenix provides `ChannelCase` for cleanly testing them without a running WebSocket server.

Example: a simple room channel:

```
defmodule MyAppWeb.RoomChannel do
  use Phoenix.Channel

  def join("room:" <> _room_id, _params, socket) do
    {:ok, socket}
  end

  def handle_in("new_message", %{"body" => body},
socket) do
    broadcast!(socket, "new_message", %{body:
body})
    {:noreply, socket}
  end
end
```

Testing the channel:

```
defmodule MyAppWeb.RoomChannelTest do
  use MyAppWeb.ChannelCase, async: true

  setup do
    {:ok, _, socket} =
      MyAppWeb.UserSocket
      |> socket("user_id", %{some: :assigns})
      |> subscribe_and_join(MyAppWeb.RoomChannel,
"room:lobby")

    %{socket: socket}
  end
```

```
  test "broadcasts messages to room", %{socket:
socket} do
    push(socket, "new_message", %{"body" =>
"Hello"})
    assert_broadcast "new_message", %{body:
"Hello"}
  end
end
```

subscribe_and_join/3 connects to the channel and joins a topic.

push/3 simulates sending an event to the server.

assert_broadcast/2 verifies that a message was broadcasted back.

Channel tests verify:

Authorization logic (who can join which topic).

Event handling behavior.

Broadcasting correctness.

Error handling when inputs are invalid.

You can also test intercepting and rebroadcasting messages between users easily.

Testing LiveViews

LiveView adds a reactive layer to Phoenix applications without heavy client-side JavaScript. Phoenix provides **LiveViewTest**, a set of helpers to render, interact with, and assert on LiveViews directly.

Example: testing a simple counter LiveView:

```
defmodule MyAppWeb.CounterLive do
  use MyAppWeb, :live_view

  def mount(_params, _session, socket) do
    {:ok, assign(socket, :count, 0)}
  end

  def handle_event("increment", _params, socket) do
```

```
      {:noreply, update(socket, :count, &(&1 + 1))}
    end
end
```

Testing the LiveView:

```
defmodule MyAppWeb.CounterLiveTest do
  use MyAppWeb.ConnCase
  import Phoenix.LiveViewTest

  test "initial render shows count and increments",
%{conn: conn} do
    {:ok, view, _html} = live(conn, "/counter")

    assert render(view) =~ "0"

    view
    |> element("button", "Increment")
    |> render_click()

    assert render(view) =~ "1"
  end
end
```

Key points:

live/2 loads the LiveView like a user navigating the browser.

element/2 targets an HTML element by tag or text.

render_click/1 simulates clicking a button or link.

render/1 captures the updated HTML after user interaction.

With LiveView testing, you can:

Assert on initial render output.

Simulate user events (clicks, forms, navigation).

Follow redirects inside LiveView flows.

Validate session and authentication behaviors.

Because LiveViewTest operates directly on server-side rendered HTML, tests are fast, deterministic, and resilient against browser quirks.

Real-World Example: User Registration Flow

Suppose you have a registration form using LiveView.

In your `RegistrationLive`, you:

Display a form.

Validate input on the fly.

Submit to create a user.

Test that the form renders and submission works:

```
defmodule MyAppWeb.RegistrationLiveTest do
  use MyAppWeb.ConnCase
  import Phoenix.LiveViewTest

  test "registers a new user", %{conn: conn} do
    {:ok, view, _html} = live(conn, "/register")

    view
    |> form("#registration-form", user: %{email:
"test@example.com", password: "password123"})
    |> render_submit()

    assert_redirect(view, "/dashboard")
  end
end
```

This simulates:

Filling in form fields.

Submitting the form.

Following the redirect if registration is successful.

You verify the entire user flow end-to-end without needing a browser.

Common Testing Patterns and Tips

Always isolate tests: don't let tests depend on external state unless necessary.

Use `async: true` whenever possible for faster test runs.

Prefer high-level feature tests (controller/channel/LiveView) to catch integration bugs early.

Use fixtures or factories (such as `ExMachina`) to set up test data consistently.

Test error flows: invalid input, unauthorized access, timeouts.

Testing controllers, channels, and LiveViews is not difficult once you know the right tools and patterns:

Use ConnCase to test controllers cleanly.

Use ChannelCase to simulate and verify real-time events.

Use LiveViewTest to simulate rich interactive UIs server-side.

With thorough testing across your Phoenix stack, you catch bugs early, document system behavior clearly, and deploy new features with confidence.

Property-Based Testing with StreamData

Property-based testing shifts how you think about testing. Instead of writing specific input/output examples, you define **properties** your code should always satisfy. Then, a testing tool automatically generates hundreds or thousands of random inputs to verify that property, trying to expose hidden bugs you might not have anticipated.

In Elixir, **StreamData** provides an excellent library for property-based testing. It integrates with ExUnit, letting you write property tests alongside your normal test cases.

Setting Up StreamData

First, you need to add `stream_data` as a test dependency.

Edit your `mix.exs`:

```
defp deps do
  [
    {:stream_data, "~> 0.5.0", only: :test}
  ]
end
```

Fetch the dependency:

```
mix deps.get
```

StreamData will now be available to your test suite.

The Basic Idea of Property-Based Testing

In normal example-based testing, you say:

When I input 2, I expect output 4.

But in property-based testing, you say:

For all integers n, doubling n should equal n + n.

Then, the testing framework generates many random integers—positive, negative, zero, large, small—and verifies your property.

If it finds a failure, it reports the smallest failing input so you can debug efficiently.

Writing a Simple Property Test

Suppose you have a simple doubling function:

```
defmodule MyApp.Math do

  def double(x), do: x + x

end
```

Now test the property that double(x) should always equal x + x:

```
defmodule MyApp.MathPropertyTest do
  use ExUnit.Case
  use ExUnitProperties

  property "doubling a number is the same as adding
it to itself" do
    check all n <- integer() do
      assert MyApp.Math.double(n) == n + n
    end
  end
end
```

206

Here's what happens:

`check all` runs the test with many different random integers.

`integer()` is a generator producing random integers (positive, negative, zero).

If any generated input breaks the assertion, the test fails and shows you the smallest failing value.

When you run:

```
mix test
```

ExUnit runs this property hundreds of times automatically.

Understanding Generators

Generators are functions that produce streams of random data.

Common built-in generators:

`integer()` → random integers

`positive_integer()` → random positive integers

`float()` → random floating-point numbers

`boolean()` → true or false

`binary()` → random binaries (raw byte strings)

`string(:alphanumeric)` → random strings of letters and numbers

`list_of(generator)` → lists containing random items

Example: generating lists of integers:

```
property "sum of a list is greater than each
element" do
  check all list <- list_of(integer(), min_length:
1) do
    total = Enum.sum(list)
    assert Enum.all?(list, fn x -> total >= x end)
  end
end
```

StreamData automatically respects options like `min_length: 1`.

Building Custom Generators

You can define complex generators for domain-specific data.

Example: a valid user registration input

```
def user_input_generator do
  map_of([
    username: string(:alphanumeric, min_length: 3),
    email: string(:alphanumeric, min_length: 5),
    age: integer(18..99)
  ])
end
```

Now you can write:

```
property "usernames are at least 3 characters long"
do
  check all user <- user_input_generator() do
    assert String.length(user.username) >= 3
  end
end
```

Custom generators are powerful for testing APIs, forms, and systems that expect structured input.

Real-World Example: Testing a Slug Generator

Suppose you have a function that generates slugs for URLs:

```
defmodule MyApp.Slugger do
  def slugify(string) do
    string
    |> String.downcase()
    |> String.replace(~r/[^a-z0-9]/, "-")
    |> String.trim("-")
  end
end
You can write property tests like:
defmodule MyApp.SluggerTest do
  use ExUnit.Case
  use ExUnitProperties
```

```
  property "slug contains only lowercase letters, numbers,
and hyphens" do
    check all text <- string(:printable) do
      slug = MyApp.Slugger.slugify(text)
      assert slug =~ ~r/^[a-z0-9-]*$/
    end
  end

  property "slug never starts or ends with hyphen" do
    check all text <- string(:printable) do
      slug = MyApp.Slugger.slugify(text)
      refute String.starts_with?(slug, "-")
      refute String.ends_with?(slug, "-")
    end
  end
end
```

Instead of testing a few fixed examples, you validate the behavior across thousands of random input strings.

You might even discover edge cases—like strings made entirely of punctuation—that you'd never have thought to test manually.

Shrinking Failures

When a property fails, StreamData **shrinks** the failing input to the simplest case that still causes the failure.

Example:

Suppose the failure originally happened on:

```
"This!!!Is___AnExample"
```

StreamData will automatically try simpler cases like:

"ThisIsAnExample"

"ThisIs"

"!!"

" "

until it finds the minimal failing input.

This makes debugging much faster because you don't have to guess which part of the input caused the issue.

When to Use Property-Based Testing

Property-based testing is most valuable when:

You have a function that manipulates structured data (lists, maps, strings, numbers).

You need to validate invariants across many possible inputs.

You want to uncover edge cases that would be tedious to think of manually.

You want to validate transformations, encoders, decoders, parsers, calculations, and business rules.

It complements, not replaces, example-based tests. Use both together for maximum confidence.

Property-based testing with StreamData takes your testing strategy beyond manual examples:

Define properties your code should always satisfy.

Generate thousands of random inputs automatically.

Discover hidden bugs and edge cases early.

Get minimized failing inputs to debug quickly.

Build stronger, more resilient systems by testing across wide input spaces.

By combining ExUnit and StreamData, you can ensure your Elixir and Phoenix applications are not only correct for a few cases but reliable across entire ranges of real-world scenarios.

Debugging and Observability Tools

No matter how carefully you design, test, and structure your Elixir and Phoenix applications, issues will eventually arise. Maybe it's a subtle bug in production, a performance bottleneck under unexpected load, or a misbehaving background process. Having robust debugging and observability practices is what separates a fragile system from one that can recover quickly and improve continuously.

Elixir and the BEAM provide exceptional tools for debugging, tracing, and observing live systems. In this section, we'll explore practical ways to debug problems and keep a close eye on your system's health through observability tools.

Using Logger for Debugging

The first and most direct tool you have is Elixir's built-in `Logger`.

You can log information at different levels:

```
Logger.debug("Debugging details", user_id: 123)

Logger.info("Normal operation", event: :login)

Logger.warn("Something looks suspicious",
attempt_count: 5)

Logger.error("Failure to process payment",
order_id: 456)
```

By default, Phoenix configures Logger to output to your console and captures useful request metadata, such as HTTP method, path, and status code.

Adjusting logging level in `config/config.exs`:

```
config :logger, level: :info
```

For deeper debugging during development, set it to `:debug`. In production, you usually stick with `:info` or `:warn` to avoid noisy logs.

Best practices for effective logging:

Always include meaningful context using metadata (e.g., `user_id`, `order_id`, `job_id`).

Log important state changes, errors, and critical decision points.

Avoid logging sensitive data like passwords or credit card numbers.

Make logs structured and machine-parseable if possible (e.g., JSON format for production systems).

Inspecting Live Systems with :observer

The BEAM comes with a powerful GUI tool called `:observer`, which gives you live insight into processes, memory usage, system load, and more.

Starting Observer in an IEx shell:

```
:observer.start()
```

The Observer dashboard allows you to:

View the running supervision tree.

Inspect all running processes and their memory usage.

See message queue lengths (important for spotting backpressure).

Watch CPU and memory charts over time.

This is invaluable for catching runaway processes, memory leaks, or bottlenecks.

Observer is best used in development or staging environments. In production, it's usually disabled or requires careful node authentication setup.

Tracing Processes with :dbg and :sys

If you need to trace how a particular process behaves without modifying the code, you can use BEAM's built-in tracing tools.

Tracing all messages received by a process:

```
pid = Process.whereis(MyApp.Worker)

:dbg.tracer()

:dbg.p(pid, [:receive])
```

Now, every message the process receives is printed to your console.

You can also use `:sys.trace(pid, true)` for slightly lighter tracing.

This is extremely useful when diagnosing why a GenServer behaves incorrectly, why certain messages aren't processed, or why a worker appears stuck.

Example: Investigating a stuck GenServer

Suppose you notice a background worker isn't making progress. By attaching a tracer:

```
:sys.get_state(pid)
```

You can inspect the current state of the process without halting it, helping you see if it's stuck on bad data or waiting on something external.

Observability with Telemetry

Elixir provides a unified event system called **Telemetry**, which libraries like Phoenix, Ecto, and Oban use internally.

You can emit your own events easily:

```
:telemetry.execute(

  [:my_app, :orders, :created],

  %{duration: 123_456},

  %{user_id: 101}

)
```

Here:

The first argument is the event name (list of atoms).

The second argument is measurements (numeric values).

The third argument is metadata (anything descriptive).

You can then attach event handlers to collect these events and export them to:

Prometheus

StatsD

Datadog

AppSignal

Honeycomb

New Relic

Example: Setting up a simple Telemetry handler

```
defmodule MyApp.TelemetryHandler do
  def attach do
    :telemetry.attach(
      "log-order-created",
      [:my_app, :orders, :created],
      &handle_order_created/4,
      nil
    )
  end

  def handle_order_created(_event, measurements,
metadata, _config) do
    Logger.info("Order created", measurements:
measurements, metadata: metadata)
  end
end
```

Call `MyApp.TelemetryHandler.attach()` in your application startup to begin listening for events.

Using Phoenix LiveDashboard

Phoenix LiveDashboard brings observability directly into your browser, with real-time metrics about your running application.

After installing and configuring it:

```
# router.ex
import Phoenix.LiveDashboard.Router

if Mix.env() in [:dev, :test] do
  scope "/" do
    pipe_through :browser
    live_dashboard "/dashboard", metrics:
MyAppWeb.Telemetry
  end
end
```

Access it at /dashboard while running your app.

LiveDashboard provides:

System metrics (CPU, memory, scheduler utilization).

Request breakdowns (response times, status codes).

Process monitoring (long queues, memory leaks).

Live inspection of running GenServers and ETS tables.

You can also integrate it with custom Telemetry metrics for domain-specific dashboards (e.g., tracking how many users are online).

Real-World Debugging Example: Slow Page Loads

Suppose your application's dashboard page starts loading slowly under high traffic.

Here's a strategy to debug it:

Check Phoenix logs: look for slow request durations and query times.

Look at LiveDashboard: inspect Ecto query timings and CPU load.

Trace long-living processes: use `:observer` or `:sys.get_state/1` to see if GenServers are holding too much state or stuck.

Add Telemetry spans around expensive operations:

```
:telemetry.span(
  [:my_app, :dashboard, :load],
  %{},
  fn ->
    data = MyApp.Stats.fetch_heavy_data()
    {data, %{item_count: length(data)}}
  end
)
```

Export metrics to Prometheus and Grafana for historical tracking.

By observing rather than guessing, you can find bottlenecks, verify fixes, and prove improvements quantitatively.

Debugging and observability are not only about fixing errors—they are about **making your systems understandable and predictable** even under stress:

Use Logger extensively with rich metadata.

Inspect live systems safely with Observer and sys tools.

Emit Telemetry events to track performance-critical actions.

Visualize system health with LiveDashboard.

Export structured metrics to external monitoring platforms.

With these techniques, you move from reactive firefighting to proactive system health management, ensuring your Elixir and Phoenix applications stay reliable, performant, and maintainable at any scale.

Chapter 11: Deploying Phoenix Applications in Production

Developing an Elixir and Phoenix application is only half the battle. To turn it into a real-world product, you need to package, configure, deploy, monitor, and maintain it in a live environment. Fortunately, the Elixir ecosystem gives you excellent tools for building robust releases, securing sensitive settings, running apps on modern hosting platforms, and observing system health through real-time telemetry.

Building Releases with Mix

Deploying a Phoenix application into production isn't just about copying your source code to a server and running `mix phx.server`. To achieve real production stability, scalability, and operational control, you need to package your app properly as a **release**. A release is a fully self-contained, compiled bundle that includes your application, its dependencies, the Erlang Virtual Machine (ERTS), and management scripts to run, restart, and introspect your system.

The Elixir build tool, **Mix**, provides a powerful built-in mechanism for building production releases. It allows you to produce a highly portable artifact that you can deploy on any Linux machine without needing to install Elixir or Erlang separately.

Why Use a Release Instead of Running Mix in Production?

Running `mix phx.server` works well in development because it gives you hot code reloading, instant recompilation, and developer conveniences. In production, however, you want:

A compiled, optimized, and minimized application.

A single start/stop point for the server and background jobs.

Control scripts for graceful shutdowns and remote IEx shells.

Security: no need for Mix, no source files, no extra tooling.

A release ensures you can move your app to any environment and operate it like a real production service, not just a development toy.

217

Preparing Your Phoenix App for Releases

Before building a release, a Phoenix app needs certain settings in place to make sure it boots correctly when it's deployed outside of your local machine.

Create or edit your `config/runtime.exs` file. This file is evaluated at runtime, allowing you to load settings from environment variables or external sources securely.

Here's a standard `runtime.exs` setup for a Phoenix project:

```elixir
import Config

if config_env() == :prod do
  database_url = System.fetch_env!("DATABASE_URL")
  secret_key_base =
System.fetch_env!("SECRET_KEY_BASE")

  config :my_app, MyApp.Repo,
    url: database_url,
    pool_size:
String.to_integer(System.get_env("POOL_SIZE") ||
"10"),
    ssl: true

  config :my_app, MyAppWeb.Endpoint,
    server: true,
    http: [
      port:
String.to_integer(System.get_env("PORT") ||
"4000"),
      transport_options: [socket_opts: [:inet6]]
    ],
    secret_key_base: secret_key_base
end
```

Key points:

`server: true` ensures that the Phoenix web server boots automatically inside the release.

Database credentials and sensitive information are pulled at runtime through environment variables.

No secrets are stored in your codebase.

If `runtime.exs` isn't properly configured, your release will boot but may not start your web endpoint, or it might crash with a missing environment variable error.

Building the Release

After ensuring your application can be configured dynamically at runtime, you can build the release.

First, make sure all dependencies are fetched and compiled for the production environment:

```
MIX_ENV=prod mix deps.get
```

```
MIX_ENV=prod mix compile
```

Now build the release:

```
MIX_ENV=prod mix release
```

When the command finishes, Mix will create a directory at:

```
_build/prod/rel/my_app/
```

Inside this folder, you will find:

A self-contained version of the Erlang runtime (`erts/`).

Your compiled app and dependencies.

Shell scripts like `bin/my_app` to start, stop, and manage your application.

This is the folder you deploy to your servers or containers.

Running the Release Locally

After building the release, you can try running it locally to ensure everything is working.

First, set the required environment variables:

```
export
DATABASE_URL="ecto://user:pass@localhost/my_app_pro
d"
```

```
export SECRET_KEY_BASE=$(mix phx.gen.secret)
```
Start the server:

```
_build/prod/rel/my_app/bin/my_app start
```

Attach to a live remote console:

```
_build/prod/rel/my_app/bin/my_app remote
```

This remote shell allows you to inspect running processes, query your database, and even hot-patch live code if necessary.

Stop the application gracefully:

```
_build/prod/rel/my_app/bin/my_app stop
```

Unlike in development mode, you don't need to install Elixir, Mix, or Erlang separately on your server because the release includes everything your app needs to run.

Customizing Release Configuration

You can define custom behavior for your release inside your mix.exs file under the :releases key.

Example:

```
def project do
  [
    app: :my_app,
    version: "0.1.0",
    releases: [
      my_app: [
        applications: [
          runtime_tools: :permanent
        ]
      ]
    ]
  ]
end
```

In this example:

The `:runtime_tools` application (which includes `:observer`, `:runtime_tools`, and `:debugger`) is bundled into the release and started permanently.

This allows you to connect to a running system and monitor live processes and memory usage.

You can further customize releases to:

Include custom boot scripts.

Run database migrations automatically after boot.

Support blue/green deployments or canary releases.

Real-World Example: Dockerizing a Phoenix Release

In many production environments, releases are deployed inside Docker containers.

A minimal production `Dockerfile` looks like this:

```
# Base image with runtime dependencies
FROM hexpm/elixir:1.15.4-erlang-26.1.2-ubuntu-
jammy-20231003

RUN apt-get update && apt-get install -y openssl
ncurses-bin

# Set working directory
WORKDIR /app

# Copy built release from host to container
COPY _build/prod/rel/my_app ./

# Set environment variables
ENV HOME=/app

# Start the application
CMD ["bin/my_app", "start"]
```

You would then:

Build the release with **mix release.**

Build your Docker image with:

```
docker build -t my_app .
```

Push to your container registry or deploy directly to your server.

Common Problems and Solutions

Problem: Release starts but server is not running.

Solution: Ensure you set `server: true` inside `runtime.exs` for your endpoint.

Problem: Application crashes at boot with missing credentials.

Solution: Check that all environment variables are correctly set before starting the release.

Problem: Release size is too big.

Solution: You can remove development/test dependencies or use `mix release --overwrite --no-compile --no-deps-check` options during your pipeline build if they are unnecessary.

Building releases with Mix transforms your Phoenix application into a production-ready, self-sufficient service:

Compiling and bundling everything ensures consistent deployment across environments.

Releases allow remote console access, control scripts, and proper lifecycle management.

Runtime configuration ensures secure, flexible environment-specific setups.

Minimal Docker images or direct server transfers make deployments lean and efficient.

By using Mix releases properly, you're preparing your application not just to run but to operate like a professional-grade production system.

Runtime Configuration and Secrets Management

When you deploy a Phoenix application into production, you can't rely on development-time configuration files like `config/dev.exs` or hardcoded values inside your project. Production environments require flexibility. Your application needs to adjust based on the server it's deployed to, the secrets it retrieves, the databases it connects to, and the scaling configuration it runs with. That's where **runtime configuration** comes in—and securely managing secrets becomes a critical part of that setup.

Elixir provides powerful tools to make your application dynamically configurable and secure at runtime, without bloating your codebase with sensitive or environment-specific logic.

The Purpose of Runtime Configuration

Runtime configuration means your application doesn't hardcode details like:

Database URLs

Encryption keys

Redis hostnames

Mail server credentials

External API tokens

Instead, it loads them **at runtime**, typically from **environment variables** that are provided when your release is deployed. This enables the same compiled release to run on staging, production, or any customer-specific environment, with the correct values injected on boot.

This approach is especially important in releases built with `mix release`, because at runtime, you can't use Mix config helpers (like `Mix.env()` or `Mix.Project.config/0`). The config has to be environment-agnostic and driven externally.

Using `runtime.exs` for Dynamic Settings

The file `config/runtime.exs` is the core of Elixir's runtime configuration system. It's evaluated at boot time of your application **after** the release has started loading, but **before** any processes (like your Phoenix endpoint or Ecto Repo) are started.

Here's a practical example:

```elixir
import Config

if config_env() == :prod do
  config :my_app, MyApp.Repo,
    url: System.fetch_env!("DATABASE_URL"),
    pool_size:
String.to_integer(System.get_env("POOL_SIZE") ||
"10"),
    ssl: true

  config :my_app, MyAppWeb.Endpoint,
    server: true,
    http: [
      port:
String.to_integer(System.get_env("PORT") || "4000")
    ],
    secret_key_base:
System.fetch_env!("SECRET_KEY_BASE")
end
```

What this does:

Loads `DATABASE_URL` and ensures it exists.

Dynamically sets the `POOL_SIZE` with a default fallback.

Turns on SSL.

Ensures Phoenix's endpoint boots in production.

Injects `SECRET_KEY_BASE`, required for session signing and secure cookies.

This file should not contain any hardcoded credentials or production-specific values. All of that should come from your environment.

You can test your runtime configuration locally with:

```
MIX_ENV=prod iex -S mix phx.server
```

Or from a release:

```
_build/prod/rel/my_app/bin/my_app start
```

If any required environment variable is missing, `System.fetch_env!/1` will raise at boot, preventing a misconfigured application from starting silently.

Securing Secrets with Environment Variables

The safest and most common approach to injecting secrets is by using **environment variables**.

Benefits:

They keep secrets outside of your source code.

They're easy to manage with CI/CD pipelines and secret managers.

They are compatible with Docker, Kubernetes, systemd, and virtually all production orchestrators.

Examples of critical secrets you should always load at runtime:

```
DATABASE_URL
```

```
SECRET_KEY_BASE
```

```
REDIS_URL
```

```
API_TOKEN
```

```
MAILGUN_API_KEY
```

You can set them in your shell:

```
export
DATABASE_URL=ecto://user:pass@localhost/my_app

export SECRET_KEY_BASE=$(mix phx.gen.secret)
```

Or manage them with `.env` files in development using a tool like `direnv` or `dotenv`.

In production (e.g., Render, Fly.io, or Gigalixir), you typically define these in your platform dashboard or deployment scripts.

Loading Structured Secrets (Optional Pattern)

If you prefer managing secrets in a single JSON blob (for example, when using Vault or fetching secrets from an external API), you can decode that blob inside `runtime.exs`.

```
import Config

if config_env() == :prod do
  secret_blob = System.fetch_env!("MY_APP_SECRETS")
  {:ok, secrets} = Jason.decode(secret_blob)

  config :my_app, MyAppWeb.Endpoint,
    secret_key_base: secrets["secret_key_base"]

  config :my_app, MyApp.Mailer,
    smtp_host: secrets["smtp_host"],
    smtp_user: secrets["smtp_user"],
    smtp_password: secrets["smtp_password"]
end
```

This allows you to centralize secrets, rotate them easily, and fetch them from encrypted external stores.

Be careful to validate that your blob is well-formed, and fail fast if it's not.

Avoiding Common Pitfalls

Here are a few traps to avoid when working with runtime config and secrets:

1. Hardcoding production secrets in `config/prod.exs`

This is dangerous. Secrets should never be stored in version control.

2. Using `Mix.env()` in `runtime.exs`

This works in dev/test configs, but it's unnecessary in `runtime.exs`—you should use `config_env()` instead, which works inside compiled releases.

3. Not setting `server: true` in the Endpoint config

Without this, your Phoenix app will boot, but the web server won't start. Always set this in `runtime.exs` for production environments.

4. Forgetting to validate required secrets

If `System.get_env/1` returns `nil`, your app might boot incorrectly. Always use `System.fetch_env!/1` when the value is required.

Real-World Example: Render Deployment

In Render, you manage secrets through the dashboard:

Go to your service > Environment.

Set:

DATABASE_URL

SECRET_KEY_BASE

PORT (Render sets this automatically)

In your `runtime.exs`, make sure you're using `System.fetch_env!`.

Render injects the secrets into your container's environment when it boots. You don't have to commit anything secret to Git.

If you're using Oban, a Redis URL, or any third-party integration, apply the same principle: define the secret externally and access it with `System.get_env/1`.

Validating Secrets in CI

To ensure your application fails early if a secret is missing, add a CI check to parse `runtime.exs` in your test pipeline and simulate booting:

```
MIX_ENV=prod mix compile
```

Or even better:

```
MIX_ENV=prod iex -S mix
```

Set fake values for secrets during CI (just enough to pass config parsing) and let your CI catch accidental errors in `runtime.exs`.

Runtime configuration and secrets management are foundational to building a secure, portable, production-grade Phoenix application. By dynamically injecting settings using environment variables, validating them on boot, and keeping secrets out of your codebase, you ensure your app:

Can run in any environment with zero config changes

Keeps sensitive credentials protected

Responds to operational changes without rebuilds

Scales safely and predictably in production

This practice, when paired with proper release building, creates a clear boundary between your source code and your deployed infrastructure—making your applications easier to operate and safer to trust.

Deploying to Fly.io, Render, and Gigalixir

Once you've built a Phoenix application and packaged it as a release, the next step is deploying it to a production-ready platform. The Elixir ecosystem offers great flexibility in this area. You can deploy to your own VPS, Docker-based orchestrators like Kubernetes, or fully managed platforms. Among the most Elixir-friendly options are **Fly.io**, **Render**, and **Gigalixir**. Each platform takes a slightly different approach, but all support seamless deployment of Phoenix applications with a strong focus on developer experience.

Deploying to Fly.io

Fly.io lets you run apps globally close to users. It's lightweight, uses Docker under the hood, and has native support for the BEAM.

Step 1 – Install Fly CLI

Fly provides a command-line tool that handles deployment and app provisioning.

```
curl -L https://fly.io/install.sh | sh
```

After installation:

```
fly auth signup
```

or

```
fly auth login
```

Step 2 – Create Your Phoenix App

Navigate to your project directory, then run:

```
fly launch
```

This walks you through setting up a Fly app, including:

Creating a `fly.toml` configuration file.

Generating a Dockerfile if you don't already have one.

Selecting a deployment region.

Step 3 – Configure Your Release and Runtime

Ensure you have `config/runtime.exs` handling your environment variables, such as:

```
config :my_app, MyApp.Repo,
  url: System.fetch_env!("DATABASE_URL"),
  pool_size:
String.to_integer(System.get_env("POOL_SIZE") ||
"10"),
  ssl: true

config :my_app, MyAppWeb.Endpoint,
  http: [
    port: String.to_integer(System.get_env("PORT")
|| "4000"),
    transport_options: [socket_opts: [:inet6]]
  ],
  secret_key_base:
System.fetch_env!("SECRET_KEY_BASE"),
  server: true
```

Step 4 – Provision a Database

You can attach a PostgreSQL database using:

```
fly postgres create
```

Link it to your app:

```
fly postgres attach --app your_app_name
```

This sets DATABASE_URL and other necessary secrets in your Fly app environment.

Step 5 – Set Secrets

Provide SECRET_KEY_BASE:

```
fly secrets set SECRET_KEY_BASE=$(mix
phx.gen.secret)
```

Step 6 – Deploy

Push your release to Fly.io:

```
fly deploy
```

Fly builds your Docker image, deploys it globally, and sets up load balancing and HTTPS automatically.

To see logs:

```
fly logs
```

To open the site:

```
fly open
```

Fly is particularly good for apps that require clustering, node distribution, or global presence, making it an ideal fit for LiveView-heavy apps or real-time apps using Phoenix Channels.

Deploying to Render

Render is a general-purpose platform-as-a-service provider with support for Elixir. It offers automatic builds from GitHub, managed databases, and a simple interface.

Step 1 – Prepare Your Phoenix App

Ensure you have a working **mix release** setup, a valid **runtime.exs** file, and that your app compiles cleanly in production mode.

In `mix.exs`, define the release:

```
releases: [
  my_app: [
    applications: [runtime_tools: :permanent]
  ]
]
```

Step 2 – Push Your Code to GitHub

Render pulls directly from GitHub repositories. Push your Phoenix app to a public or private repo.

Step 3 – Set Up a PostgreSQL Database

Render offers a one-click PostgreSQL service. Create one and copy the `DATABASE_URL` it provides.

Step 4 – Create a Web Service

Go to **Dashboard > New > Web Service**.

Choose your Phoenix repo.

Set:

Build Command:

```
mix deps.get && mix compile && mix assets.deploy &&
mix release
```

Start Command:

```
_build/prod/rel/my_app/bin/my_app start
```

Set environment variables:

DATABASE_URL

SECRET_KEY_BASE

MIX_ENV=prod

Step 5 – Configure the Port

Render assigns port `10000` internally. Update your `runtime.exs` accordingly:

231

```
config :my_app, MyAppWeb.Endpoint,
  http: [ip: {0, 0, 0, 0}, port:
String.to_integer(System.get_env("PORT") ||
"10000")],
  secret_key_base:
System.fetch_env!("SECRET_KEY_BASE"),
  server: true
```

Step 6 – Deploy Automatically

Render detects pushes to your GitHub repository and deploys automatically. Logs and status are available in the dashboard.

Render is a good option when you want fast setup, auto-scaling, and no DevOps headaches. It's ideal for apps where convenience matters more than fine-grained control.

Deploying to Gigalixir

Gigalixir is a platform-as-a-service built specifically for Elixir and Phoenix applications. It supports clustering, hot upgrades, and zero-downtime deploys natively.

Step 1 – Install CLI

```
pip install gigalixir --upgrade
```

Then:

```
gigalixir login
```

Step 2 – Create an App

```
gigalixir apps:create my_app_name
```

Step 3 – Add a Database

```
gigalixir pg:create --free
```

This attaches a free PostgreSQL instance and sets DATABASE_URL.

Step 4 – Add Secrets

```
gigalixir secrets:set SECRET_KEY_BASE=$(mix
phx.gen.secret)
```

232

Step 5 – Configure Your Phoenix App

You must enable releases in `mix.exs` and configure the `runtime.exs` just like before. Ensure you use `server: true`.

Additionally, set the release to run migrations automatically after deploy, either through release hooks or a dedicated command.

Step 6 – Deploy

Deploy using Git:

```
git remote add gigalixir
https://username@gigalixir.com/my_app_name.git
git push gigalixir main
```

Gigalixir will:

Build your app using a pre-configured Elixir buildpack.

Boot the release automatically.

Provide TLS and scaling options out of the box.

Use:

```
gigalixir logs
```

to tail your logs in real time.

Gigalixir is great for apps that need distributed features of the BEAM like PubSub clustering, hot code upgrades, and native Erlang observability tools.

Deployment Comparison

Feature	Fly.io	Render	Gigalixir
Native BEAM support	Yes	Partial	Full
Clustering support	Yes	No	Yes
Built-in Postgres	Yes	Yes	Yes

233

Feature	Fly.io	Render	Gigalixir
Hot upgrades	Manual	No	Yes
Web-based setup	Optional	Required	Optional
Docker required	Yes (default)	Optional	No

Each platform—Fly.io, Render, and Gigalixir—offers a strong deployment experience for Phoenix apps. The best choice depends on what you're optimizing for:

Use **Fly.io** when you want full control over infrastructure, edge deployment, and global scalability.

Choose **Render** for an ultra-simple GitOps workflow with minimal setup.

Go with **Gigalixir** if you want Elixir-native clustering, built-in hot upgrades, and minimal ops for BEAM-specific features.

Regardless of platform, focus on building clean releases, managing secrets securely with runtime config, and using observability tools to monitor your deployment after it's live.

Monitoring, Metrics, and Alerts with Telemetry

Building and deploying a Phoenix application is not complete without setting up proper monitoring. In production, you need to know how your system behaves over time, spot performance bottlenecks early, detect system failures, and be alerted before users notice problems. Telemetry is the cornerstone of monitoring in Elixir and Phoenix applications, giving you a standardized way to collect operational metrics, analyze performance, and set up actionable alerts.

What Is Telemetry?

Telemetry is a lightweight event dispatching system used throughout the Elixir ecosystem. It allows libraries (like Ecto, Phoenix, or Oban) and your own application code to emit structured events about what's happening inside the system.

Each telemetry event has:

Name: a list of atoms that uniquely identifies the event, like `[:phoenix, :endpoint, :start]`.

Measurements: a map of quantitative data like timing, counts, or byte sizes.

Metadata: a map of contextual information like user IDs, request paths, or query strings.

Telemetry does not persist data or export it by itself. It simply emits the events. You decide what to do with them by attaching **handlers**.

This design keeps Telemetry extremely lightweight and composable, even at high volumes.

Where Telemetry Events Come From

Out of the box, several core libraries in Phoenix applications emit telemetry events:

Phoenix Endpoint: request durations, response status codes.

Ecto: database query timings, success/failure stats.

Oban: job execution metrics, retry counts.

LiveView: mount and event handling timings.

You can also emit custom telemetry events in your own code easily.

Example:

```
:telemetry.execute(
  [:my_app, :user, :signed_in],
  %{count: 1},
  %{user_id: 123}
)
```

This event signals that a user signed in, including the user's ID for context.

Attaching Telemetry Handlers

To do something useful with telemetry events (like exporting metrics to Prometheus or Datadog), you need to attach a handler.

Handlers are simple Elixir modules or functions that react to telemetry events.

Example handler:

```
defmodule MyApp.TelemetryHandlers do

  def handle_user_signed_in(_event_name,
measurements, metadata, _config) do

    IO.inspect({measurements, metadata}, label:
"User signed in")

  end
end
```

Attach the handler when your application boots:

```
:telemetry.attach(

  "log-user-signed-in",

  [:my_app, :user, :signed_in],

  &MyApp.TelemetryHandlers.handle_user_signed_in/4,

  nil

)
```

Now, every time a user signs in, the handler will log the event.

You can attach multiple handlers to the same event, or filter which events you want to listen to.

Exporting Metrics to Monitoring Systems

In production, you typically want to export telemetry events to a time-series database and visualize them using dashboards.

Popular choices:

Prometheus + Grafana: Open-source, widely used.

Datadog: SaaS monitoring with strong Elixir support.

AppSignal, **New Relic**, **Honeycomb**: Commercial services with Elixir agents.

To bridge Telemetry events to these systems, you often use libraries like:

```
telemetry_metrics

telemetry_metrics_prometheus

telemetry_metrics_datadog
```

Example: setting up Prometheus exporter

First, add dependencies:

```
defp deps do
  [
    {:telemetry_metrics, "~> 0.6"},
    {:telemetry_metrics_prometheus, "~> 1.0"},
    {:prometheus_ex, "~> 3.0"}
  ]
end
```

Then, define a metrics module:

```
defmodule MyAppWeb.Telemetry do
  use Supervisor

  import Telemetry.Metrics

  def start_link(_arg) do
    Supervisor.start_link(__MODULE__, :ok, name:
__MODULE__)
  end

  def init(:ok) do
    children = [
      {TelemetryMetricsPrometheus, metrics:
metrics()}
    ]
```

```
    Supervisor.init(children, strategy:
:one_for_one)
  end

  def metrics do
    [
      counter("phoenix.endpoint.stop.count"),
      summary("phoenix.endpoint.stop.duration",
        unit: {:native, :millisecond}
      ),
      summary("ecto.query.total_time",
        unit: {:native, :millisecond}
      )
    ]
  end
end
```

Mount a `/metrics` endpoint to expose the metrics:

```
scope "/" do

  pipe_through :browser

  forward "/metrics", TelemetryMetricsPrometheus

end
```

Now Prometheus can scrape metrics from your Phoenix app at `/metrics`.

Designing Effective Alerts

Collecting metrics is only the first step. To keep your app reliable, you must create alerts that warn you early about problems.

Good alerting focuses on:

Latency: response times growing over thresholds.

Error rates: HTTP 500s, DB failures, background job retries.

Resource exhaustion: CPU saturation, memory leaks, process queue build-up.

Availability: service downtime or unreachable endpoints.

Examples of alert thresholds:

5% of HTTP requests return 5xx errors in 5 minutes.

Database query duration exceeds 500ms average.

Background job retries exceed 10% over 15 minutes.

In Prometheus, you might define alerts like:

```
groups:
  - name: phoenix.rules
    rules:
    - alert: HighErrorRate
      expr:
sum(rate(phoenix_http_requests_total{status=~"5.."}
[5m]))
              /
sum(rate(phoenix_http_requests_total[5m])) > 0.05
      for: 5m
      labels:
        severity: critical
      annotations:
        description: "High error rate detected in the
last 5 minutes."
```

For Datadog or AppSignal, similar thresholds can be set through their UI.

Alert Design Tip: Always tune your alerts to minimize noise. Flapping alerts cause engineers to ignore real incidents. Aggregate and smooth metrics where possible.

Adding Telemetry to Your Own Application Logic

Besides using telemetry from Phoenix and Ecto, you should instrument your own critical paths:

User registration

Payment processing

External API calls

Complex background tasks

Example: instrumenting a long-running task:

239

```
defmodule MyApp.BackgroundTasks do
  def process_order(order_id) do
    :telemetry.span(
      [:my_app, :order, :process],
      %{},
      fn ->
        result = do_order_processing(order_id)
        {result, %{order_id: order_id}}
      end
    )
  end
end
```

The `:telemetry.span/3` function automatically captures start/stop timing and emits a structured event.

This gives you full visibility into how long real-world operations take, and where bottlenecks occur.

Real-World Example: Monitoring a LiveView Application

Suppose you have a LiveView-powered dashboard for your users. You care about:

Page load times (LiveView mount durations)

User interaction responsiveness (event handling durations)

Error tracking (failed event handlers)

You can:

Capture `phoenix_live_view.mount.stop.duration` to monitor page loads.

Measure `phoenix_live_view.handle_event.stop.duration` to catch slow UX events.

Set up alerts if mounting takes more than 2 seconds, indicating database or API issues.

By surfacing this telemetry into Prometheus or Datadog, you know instantly whether users are having a fast or frustrating experience.

Monitoring, metrics, and alerts are essential for running Phoenix applications at production quality:

Telemetry provides a lightweight, powerful way to emit and collect operational events.

Handlers and exporters let you feed telemetry into visualization and alerting systems.

Effective alerting focuses on service-level behavior: latency, errors, and availability.

Instrumenting your application code gives deeper insights beyond system metrics.

A properly monitored system doesn't just run—it tells you when it's struggling, where it's hurting, and gives you a chance to fix problems before your users even notice.

Chapter 12: Beyond the Basics: APIs, GraphQL, and More

By now, you've seen how Phoenix excels at building full-stack web applications with real-time features. But Phoenix is just as powerful when used as a pure backend service for APIs. Whether you're serving traditional REST APIs, building flexible GraphQL endpoints, or streaming real-time data to clients, Phoenix gives you the tools to design scalable and maintainable backend architectures.

This chapter focuses on building production-quality APIs with Phoenix, introduces the Absinthe GraphQL framework, explains how to use GraphQL subscriptions for real-time updates, and shows how to configure Phoenix for API-only applications when you don't need server-rendered HTML.

Building APIs with Phoenix

When you're building modern software applications—whether for mobile, web, or microservices—your backend needs to be efficient, scalable, and easy to maintain. Phoenix, built on the Elixir language and the BEAM virtual machine, gives you exactly that. With its first-class support for functional programming, concurrency, and fault tolerance, Phoenix also makes API development a pleasure rather than a chore.

Let's walk through building a RESTful JSON API using Phoenix step by step, starting with routing, controllers, views, data serialization, and best practices for versioning, authentication, and error handling. By the end, you'll have a fully functional and idiomatic Phoenix API that meets professional production standards.

Starting with a Clean Phoenix API Project

You can use Phoenix in a full-stack mode with LiveView and HTML rendering, but for a clean API-centric project, you typically disable HTML and asset generation. You can do this from the start:

```
mix phx.new tasks_api --no-html --no-assets
cd tasks_api
mix ecto.create
```

This sets up a lean Phoenix project focused solely on serving JSON responses. You still get everything you need: routers, controllers, Ecto integration, and Plug middleware.

Defining Routes and the API Pipeline

Phoenix uses a layered approach for routing. At the outer layer, you define your request pipeline and how requests flow through the router.

Here's how to set up a scoped API version with JSON-only handling:

```
# lib/tasks_api_web/router.ex
defmodule TasksApiWeb.Router do
  use TasksApiWeb, :router

  pipeline :api do
    plug :accepts, ["json"]
  end

  scope "/api/v1", TasksApiWeb do
    pipe_through :api

    resources "/tasks", TaskController, except:
[:new, :edit]
  end
end
```

The `:api` pipeline configures Phoenix to only accept JSON. It skips layout rendering and asset handling entirely, giving you a pure JSON interface.

Creating the Context and Schema

Phoenix promotes a clean architecture by separating business logic into **contexts**. Let's generate a `Tasks` context to manage our task entities.

```
mix phx.gen.context Tasks Task tasks title:string
completed:boolean
```

This command scaffolds everything: the schema, migrations, and basic CRUD functions. Then run the migration:

```
mix ecto.migrate
```

You now have a `Task` schema and a `Tasks` module with useful functions like `list_tasks`, `get_task!`, `create_task`, `update_task`, and `delete_task`.

Building the TaskController

With the data layer in place, you can write a controller that exposes your API.

```elixir
# lib/tasks_api_web/controllers/task_controller.ex
defmodule TasksApiWeb.TaskController do
  use TasksApiWeb, :controller

  alias TasksApi.Tasks
  alias TasksApi.Tasks.Task

  action_fallback TasksApiWeb.FallbackController

  def index(conn, _params) do
    tasks = Tasks.list_tasks()
    render(conn, "index.json", tasks: tasks)
  end

  def show(conn, %{"id" => id}) do
    task = Tasks.get_task!(id)
    render(conn, "show.json", task: task)
  end

  def create(conn, %{"task" => task_params}) do
    with {:ok, %Task{} = task} <-
Tasks.create_task(task_params) do
      conn
      |> put_status(:created)
      |> put_resp_header("location",
Routes.task_path(conn, :show, task))
      |> render("show.json", task: task)
    end
  end

  def update(conn, %{"id" => id, "task" =>
task_params}) do
    task = Tasks.get_task!(id)

    with {:ok, %Task{} = updated_task} <-
Tasks.update_task(task, task_params) do
```

244

```
      render(conn, "show.json", task: updated_task)
    end
  end

  def delete(conn, %{"id" => id}) do
    task = Tasks.get_task!(id)

    with {:ok, %Task{}} <- Tasks.delete_task(task)
do
      send_resp(conn, :no_content, "")
    end
  end
end
```

This controller handles the full lifecycle: list, create, read, update, and delete. Each function delegates to the context and renders structured JSON responses.

Using Views for JSON Serialization

Phoenix Views aren't just for HTML — they're also used for cleanly formatting JSON output.

```
# lib/tasks_api_web/views/task_view.ex
defmodule TasksApiWeb.TaskView do
  use TasksApiWeb, :view

  def render("index.json", %{tasks: tasks}) do
    %{data: render_many(tasks, __MODULE__,
"task.json")}
  end

  def render("show.json", %{task: task}) do
    %{data: render_one(task, __MODULE__,
"task.json")}
  end

  def render("task.json", %{task: task}) do
    %{
      id: task.id,
      title: task.title,
      completed: task.completed
    }
  end
```

```
| end                                                      |
```

This approach separates data formatting from your controller logic, improving modularity and testability.

Handling Errors Gracefully with FallbackController

Rather than manually handling every error in every action, you can define a fallback controller:

```
#
lib/tasks_api_web/controllers/fallback_controller.e
x
defmodule TasksApiWeb.FallbackController do
  use TasksApiWeb, :controller

  def call(conn, {:error, %Ecto.Changeset{} =
changeset}) do
    conn
    |> put_status(:unprocessable_entity)
    |> put_view(TasksApiWeb.ChangesetView)
    |> render("error.json", changeset: changeset)
  end

  def call(conn, {:error, :not_found}) do
    conn
    |> put_status(:not_found)
    |> put_view(TasksApiWeb.ErrorView)
    |> render("404.json")
  end
end
```

And define a `ChangesetView` to transform validation errors:

```
# lib/tasks_api_web/views/changeset_view.ex
defmodule TasksApiWeb.ChangesetView do
  use TasksApiWeb, :view

  def render("error.json", %{changeset: changeset})
do
    %{errors:
Ecto.Changeset.traverse_errors(changeset,
&translate_error/1)}
```

```
    end
end
```

This centralized approach makes your API consistent and easy to extend.

Authentication and Security Considerations

For APIs exposed to the public or restricted to authenticated users, you'll likely want to add token-based authentication. Phoenix integrates well with `Guardian`, a JWT-based authentication library. You can write a custom plug to decode and verify tokens and insert that plug into your API pipeline.

Rate limiting, CORS headers, and HTTPS redirection should also be considered and handled appropriately via Plug middleware or deployment-level configuration.

Versioning Your API

As your application grows, you'll need to introduce breaking changes without affecting older clients. Phoenix makes versioning easy by namespacing your routes and controllers:

```
scope "/api/v2", TasksApiWeb.V2, as: :v2 do
  pipe_through :api
  resources "/tasks", TaskController
end
```

You can maintain V1 and V2 side-by-side while phasing out older versions over time.

Real-World Use Case: Task API for a Mobile App

Let's say you're building a mobile productivity app. The Phoenix API serves the backend. Your endpoints would look like:

GET /api/v1/tasks – List tasks

POST /api/v1/tasks – Create a new task

PUT /api/v1/tasks/:id – Update an existing task

DELETE /api/v1/tasks/:id – Delete a task

You can use tools like Postman or HTTPie to test each endpoint:

```
http POST :4000/api/v1/tasks task:='{"title": "Write Elixir book", "completed": false}'
```

Responses are always consistent, JSON-formatted, and use appropriate HTTP status codes.

Building APIs with Phoenix is efficient, scalable, and cleanly organized. You separate business logic, format responses professionally, handle errors centrally, and prepare your API for real-world consumption. Whether you're building a backend for a mobile app, web frontend, or even exposing services to third parties, Phoenix gives you everything you need—and nothing you don't.

GraphQL with Absinthe

If you're building an API where clients need flexibility to request exactly the data they want, GraphQL offers a more dynamic and efficient alternative to REST. In Elixir, the most mature and widely adopted GraphQL toolkit is **Absinthe**. It integrates seamlessly with Phoenix, supports subscriptions for real-time features, and lets you build fully-typed APIs that align closely with your application logic.

In this section, you'll learn how to set up Absinthe from scratch in a Phoenix project, define GraphQL schemas and resolvers, and expose queries and mutations in a way that's idiomatic and maintainable. We'll also cover real-world practices for structuring your schema and handling common scenarios like input validation and query complexity.

Installing Absinthe and Dependencies

To get started with Absinthe in your Phoenix project, you'll need a few packages added to your dependencies in `mix.exs`.

```
defp deps do
  [
    {:absinthe, "~> 1.7"},
    {:absinthe_plug, "~> 1.5"},
    {:absinthe_ecto, "~> 0.1.3"},
    {:plug_cowboy, "~> 2.6"},
    {:ecto_sql, "~> 3.10"} # if not already present
```

```
  ]
end
```

After updating dependencies, fetch them:

```
mix deps.get
```

Once installed, you can expose the GraphQL endpoint via your router.

Adding the GraphQL Endpoint

Open your `router.ex` and mount the GraphQL and optional GraphiQL endpoints:

```
# lib/my_app_web/router.ex
scope "/api" do
  pipe_through :api

  forward "/graphql", Absinthe.Plug, schema:
MyAppWeb.Schema
  forward "/graphiql", Absinthe.Plug.GraphiQL,
    schema: MyAppWeb.Schema,
    interface: :playground
end
```

The `/graphql` endpoint will be used for real clients and production requests, while `/graphiql` gives you a convenient in-browser IDE for testing queries.

Defining Your GraphQL Schema

All GraphQL APIs in Absinthe are defined using a schema module. This schema includes your query and mutation types, and it connects the GraphQL structure to your actual application logic through resolvers.

Let's define a basic schema for a `Task` object.

```
# lib/my_app_web/schema.ex
defmodule MyAppWeb.Schema do
  use Absinthe.Schema

  alias MyAppWeb.Resolvers

  object :task do
    field :id, :id
```

249

```
    field :title, :string
    field :completed, :boolean
  end

  query do
    field :tasks, list_of(:task) do
      resolve &Resolvers.TaskResolver.list_tasks/3
    end

    field :task, :task do
      arg :id, non_null(:id)
      resolve &Resolvers.TaskResolver.get_task/3
    end
  end

  mutation do
    field :create_task, :task do
      arg :title, non_null(:string)

      resolve &Resolvers.TaskResolver.create_task/3
    end

    field :update_task, :task do
      arg :id, non_null(:id)
      arg :title, :string
      arg :completed, :boolean

      resolve &Resolvers.TaskResolver.update_task/3
    end

    field :delete_task, :task do
      arg :id, non_null(:id)

      resolve &Resolvers.TaskResolver.delete_task/3
    end
  end
end
```

You now have a GraphQL API that supports fetching tasks, creating them, updating them, and deleting them.

Creating the Resolvers

Resolvers are regular Elixir functions that receive the query arguments and return a result, usually from your context modules.

Here's a resolver module for the Task operations:

```elixir
# lib/my_app_web/resolvers/task_resolver.ex
defmodule MyAppWeb.Resolvers.TaskResolver do
  alias MyApp.Tasks

  def list_tasks(_, _, _) do
    {:ok, Tasks.list_tasks()}
  end

  def get_task(_, %{id: id}, _) do
    case Tasks.get_task(id) do
      nil -> {:error, "Task not found"}
      task -> {:ok, task}
    end
  end

  def create_task(_, %{title: title}, _) do
    Tasks.create_task(%{title: title})
  end

  def update_task(_, %{id: id} = args, _) do
    with task when not is_nil(task) <-
Tasks.get_task(id),
         {:ok, updated} <- Tasks.update_task(task,
Map.delete(args, :id)) do
      {:ok, updated}
    else
      nil -> {:error, "Task not found"}
      {:error, changeset} -> {:error, changeset}
    end
  end

  def delete_task(_, %{id: id}, _) do
    with task when not is_nil(task) <-
Tasks.get_task(id),
         {:ok, deleted} <- Tasks.delete_task(task)
do
      {:ok, deleted}
    else
```

```
      _ -> {:error, "Could not delete task"}
    end
  end
end
```

Notice how the logic is clear, easy to test, and separated from your schema definitions. Errors are returned in a format that Absinthe can handle gracefully.

Running GraphQL Queries

With everything wired up, you can test your API using the GraphiQL interface or any GraphQL client.

Here's a sample query to fetch tasks:

```
query {
  tasks {
    id
    title
    completed
  }
}
```

A mutation to create a task:

```
mutation {
  createTask(title: "Learn Absinthe") {
    id
    title
    completed
  }
}
```

You'll receive a structured JSON response tailored exactly to the fields requested—no more, no less.

Handling Validation Errors with Changesets

Absinthe automatically transforms `{:error, changeset}` results into a usable error structure. You can further customize this by using middleware or centralized error views.

To help the client display meaningful messages, you can define a helper function like this:

```
defmodule MyAppWeb.Resolvers.Helpers do
  def format_errors(changeset) do
    Ecto.Changeset.traverse_errors(changeset, fn
{msg, opts} ->
      Enum.reduce(opts, msg, fn {key, value}, acc -
>
        String.replace(acc, "%{#{key}}",
to_string(value))
      end)
    end)
  end
end
```

This gives you cleaner control over how changeset errors appear in your API responses.

Best Practices for Structuring Your Schema

As your API grows, your schema can become difficult to manage if everything is in a single module. Absinthe supports schema modularization using `import_types/1`.

Split your object types into separate files:

```
# lib/my_app_web/schema/types/task_types.ex
defmodule MyAppWeb.Schema.Types.TaskTypes do
  use Absinthe.Schema.Notation

  object :task do
    field :id, :id
    field :title, :string
    field :completed, :boolean
  end
end
```

Then import the type in your root schema:

```
import_types MyAppWeb.Schema.Types.TaskTypes
```

This keeps your code clean and maintainable as more types are added.

Real-World Example: A Task Management Mobile Client

Let's say your mobile app needs to fetch incomplete tasks and display them. With REST, you'd need to create a custom endpoint or overload the URL with filters. With GraphQL, your query can be specific:

```
query {

  tasks {

    id

    title

    completed

  }

}
```

If you want to only show the task title and ID, you change the query without touching the backend.

GraphQL with Absinthe in Phoenix gives you a powerful, strongly typed, and flexible API system that integrates smoothly into your Elixir application. It eliminates over-fetching, reduces the number of client-server interactions, and gives clients precise control over the data they receive. Using Absinthe's schema and resolver structure, you can keep your code modular, readable, and scalable for years to come.

Real-Time APIs with GraphQL Subscriptions

In many modern applications, data doesn't just change occasionally—it changes continuously. Messaging apps, collaborative editors, live dashboards, multiplayer games, and notification systems all require real-time updates. You could handle this using Phoenix Channels directly, but Absinthe allows you to stay within the GraphQL ecosystem by supporting **subscriptions**.

With **Absinthe Subscriptions**, clients can subscribe to events like `taskCreated` or `messageReceived`, and the server will push updates as those events occur—without needing polling. Absinthe handles the plumbing by integrating with Phoenix PubSub and sockets behind the scenes.

Setting Up Your Phoenix Endpoint and Socket for Subscriptions

Subscriptions rely on WebSockets. To enable this, you first need to ensure that your Phoenix endpoint is configured to accept WebSocket connections.

In your `endpoint.ex` file:

```
# lib/my_app_web/endpoint.ex

socket "/socket", MyAppWeb.UserSocket,

  websocket: true,

  longpoll: false
```

This makes your app listen for WebSocket connections at `/socket`. You'll also want to include Absinthe's socket handler:

```
# lib/my_app_web/channels/user_socket.ex
defmodule MyAppWeb.UserSocket do
  use Phoenix.Socket
  use Absinthe.Phoenix.Socket, schema:
MyAppWeb.Schema

  channel "__absinthe__:control",
Absinthe.Phoenix.Channel

  def connect(_params, socket, _connect_info) do
    {:ok, socket}
  end

  def id(_socket), do: nil
end
```

Absinthe uses this internal `__absinthe__:control` channel to manage subscription data flow.

Enabling Absinthe Subscriptions in the Endpoint

255

Still in your `endpoint.ex`, plug in Absinthe for subscription tracking:

```
use Phoenix.Endpoint, otp_app: :my_app

plug Plug.Parsers,
  parsers: [:urlencoded, :multipart, :json],
  json_decoder: Phoenix.json_library()

# Add this line for Absinthe subscription support
use Absinthe.Phoenix.Endpoint
```

This ensures the endpoint has the lifecycle behavior needed to manage and broadcast GraphQL subscriptions.

Configuring PubSub for Local Development

In your app config (usually in `config/config.exs`), configure Phoenix PubSub:

```
config :my_app, MyAppWeb.Endpoint,

  pubsub_server: MyApp.PubSub
```

Your application module should also start the PubSub process:

```
# lib/my_app/application.ex

children = [

  MyApp.Repo,

  MyAppWeb.Telemetry,

  {Phoenix.PubSub, name: MyApp.PubSub},

  MyAppWeb.Endpoint

]
```

This sets up everything required for real-time broadcasting between processes.

Defining a GraphQL Subscription in Your Schema

Subscriptions look just like queries or mutations in your Absinthe schema, but they are defined in a `subscription` block.

Let's say we want to notify subscribers when a new task is created.

```
# lib/my_app_web/schema.ex
subscription do
  field :task_created, :task do
    config(fn _, _ ->
      {:ok, topic: "*"}
    end)
  end
end
```

The `topic` acts like a PubSub channel. For now, we use a wildcard to broadcast to all subscribers. You can scope it later for more fine-grained control.

Publishing Subscription Events

Now you need to publish events whenever a task is created. This usually happens inside your resolver, right after the task is created.

```
# lib/my_app_web/resolvers/task_resolver.ex

def create_task(_, %{title: title}, _) do

  with {:ok, task} <- Tasks.create_task(%{title: title}) do


Absinthe.Subscription.publish(MyAppWeb.Endpoint,
task, task_created: "*")

    {:ok, task}

  end

end
```

The `publish/3` function takes the endpoint, the payload (in this case, the created task), and the topic identifier defined in the schema.

Every client that has subscribed to the `task_created` field on topic * will immediately receive the task data.

Subscribing from a Client

GraphQL subscriptions require a WebSocket-based transport. The standard in the ecosystem is Apollo Client. Here's an example subscription query a client would send:

```
subscription {
  taskCreated {
    id
    title
    completed
  }
}
```

As soon as a new task is created in your system, any connected clients will instantly receive the payload pushed from the server.

This eliminates the need for polling and reduces server load dramatically.

Real-World Use Case: Real-Time Task Updates in a Team App

Let's say you're building a team task management app, and your frontend has a dashboard showing all tasks in a project. With subscriptions, users can leave the dashboard open and receive updates as new tasks are created by teammates, without needing to refresh.

This enhances user experience, reduces backend API calls, and makes your application feel responsive and modern.

Topic-Based Filtering for More Precise Broadcasting

Broadcasting to * is simple, but in real-world apps, you usually want scoped subscriptions.

For example, you can publish events based on a project ID:

```
config(fn %{project_id: project_id}, _info ->
  {:ok, topic: "project:#{project_id}"}
end)
```

Then in your resolver:

```
Absinthe.Subscription.publish(
```

```
  MyAppWeb.Endpoint,
  task,
  task_created: "project:#{task.project_id}"
)
```

This ensures users only get notifications relevant to the projects they are viewing.

Error Handling and Subscription Lifecycle

If something goes wrong during a subscription, Absinthe will return an error at the connection level. You can also use middleware or guards in your `config/2` function to verify permissions, validate the topic, or reject invalid input.

For example, you might reject a subscription if the user doesn't have access to the given project:

```
config(fn %{project_id: pid}, %{context:
%{current_user: user}} ->
  if ProjectAccess.allowed?(user, pid) do
    {:ok, topic: "project:#{pid}"}
  else
    {:error, "Unauthorized"}
  end
end)
```

This provides a natural access control mechanism during the subscription handshake.

Testing Subscriptions

Subscription testing requires maintaining a socket connection. Absinthe provides test helpers in `Absinthe.Phoenix.SubscriptionTest`, which let you simulate both the publish and subscribe sides of the channel.

You can also write integration tests using `Phoenix.ChannelTest` to assert that clients receive expected messages when mutations occur.

GraphQL Subscriptions with Absinthe give you real-time communication capabilities baked into the same schema and resolvers you use for queries and mutations. This leads to unified code, consistent APIs, and powerful user experiences. By building on top of Phoenix PubSub and the BEAM's concurrency model, Absinthe ensures that your real-time features are both scalable and fault-tolerant.

Phoenix API-Only Applications

Sometimes, your Phoenix application doesn't need to render HTML, manage templates, or compile assets. Maybe you're building a backend for a mobile app, a frontend powered by React or Vue, or a system meant only for machine-to-machine communication. In these cases, maintaining HTML views, asset pipelines, and LiveView endpoints only adds complexity.

Phoenix makes it easy to run in **API-only mode**—a stripped-down configuration focused purely on receiving requests and returning JSON. It's fast, minimal, and production-ready.

Creating a Phoenix Project Without HTML or Assets

When generating a new Phoenix app intended purely as an API, you'll want to exclude all the HTML and frontend boilerplate. Use the `--no-html` and `--no-assets` flags:

```
mix phx.new contacts_api --no-html --no-assets
```

This creates a Phoenix project without views, templates, LiveView, or webpack. It's fully focused on your backend logic.

Once created, navigate into the project and install dependencies:

```
cd contacts_api

mix deps.get
```

Then create the database:

```
mix ecto.create
```

Understanding the Structure of an API-Only Phoenix App

An API-only Phoenix app still gives you the same foundational pieces: routing, controllers, contexts, schemas, and middleware (plugs). What it doesn't include is anything related to rendering HTML or managing static assets.

Here's what's still in place:

A Router module for defining API routes.

Controller modules that handle requests.

Context modules that encapsulate business logic.

Ecto schemas and migrations for data modeling.

A clean plug pipeline optimized for JSON.

Full support for middleware, sockets, and PubSub if you want it.

This means you're not working with a special or limited mode—you're working with full Phoenix, simply configured for API use.

Configuring the JSON-Only Pipeline

In `lib/contacts_api_web/router.ex`, you'll see the default API pipeline:

```
pipeline :api do

  plug :accepts, ["json"]

end
```

This ensures your application responds only to requests with an `Accept: application/json` header and that it parses incoming JSON payloads into Elixir maps for you to use in your controllers.

This pipeline should be used in all your routes:

```
scope "/api", ContactsApiWeb do
  pipe_through :api

  resources "/contacts", ContactController, except:
[:new, :edit]
end
```

Routes like `/api/contacts` will now respond exclusively with JSON, and no HTML rendering paths are available.

Generating Contexts, Schemas, and Controllers

Let's say your API needs to manage a list of contacts. You can generate everything with:

```
mix phx.gen.json Contacts Contact contacts
name:string phone:string email:string
```

This command creates:

A context module: `Contacts`

A schema module: `Contact`

A controller: `ContactController`

A view for JSON rendering: `ContactView`

A migration file

Updates to your router to expose RESTful endpoints

Run your migration:

```
mix ecto.migrate
```

Your application now has a working JSON API with full CRUD support for contacts.

Inspecting the Controller and JSON View

The generated controller is optimized for API use, leveraging `render/3` for consistent JSON responses:

```
def index(conn, _params) do
  contacts = Contacts.list_contacts()
  render(conn, "index.json", contacts: contacts)
end
```

The associated view:

```
def render("index.json", %{contacts: contacts}) do
  %{data: render_many(contacts, __MODULE__,
"contact.json")}
end
```

```
def render("contact.json", %{contact: contact}) do
  %{
    id: contact.id,
    name: contact.name,
    phone: contact.phone,
    email: contact.email
  }
end
```

This structure ensures the data sent to the client is consistent, shaped by you, and easy to test.

Securing an API-Only Application

When you remove browser-focused features, you also remove built-in protections like CSRF. For an API that's stateless and doesn't rely on cookies, this is fine. But you still need to think about other concerns:

Authentication: Use token-based authentication (JWT, Guardian, OAuth).

Rate Limiting: Use Plug or a reverse proxy (like Nginx) to limit abuse.

CORS: If the API is being accessed from browsers, configure CORS using cors_plug.

Here's an example CORS setup in your endpoint:

```
plug CORSPlug,

  origin: ["https://myfrontend.com"],

  methods: ["GET", "POST", "PUT", "DELETE"]
```

Handling Errors Properly

Instead of returning raw errors or crashing the connection, your controllers should delegate to a fallback controller that formats errors in a predictable structure.

Phoenix provides a nice pattern using action_fallback:

```
action_fallback ContactsApiWeb.FallbackController
```

263

Your fallback controller catches cases like:

```
def call(conn, {:error, %Ecto.Changeset{} =
changeset}) do

  conn

  |> put_status(:unprocessable_entity)

  |> put_view(ContactsApiWeb.ChangesetView)

  |> render("error.json", changeset: changeset)

end
```

This guarantees that even errors follow a clean, JSON-based structure.

Deploying an API-Only Phoenix App

When it's time to deploy, you don't need to worry about asset compilation. Your release is smaller, faster to build, and easier to configure. You can deploy to any platform that supports Elixir:

Fly.io

Gigalixir

Render

Docker-based VPS

Self-hosted servers

Since you're not bundling assets, you don't need Node.js or any frontend build tools.

Use Case: Backend for a Mobile App

Let's say you're developing a mobile contacts manager app using React Native. Your Phoenix API-only backend will serve the frontend with:

A list of contacts (`GET /api/contacts`)

Create contact (`POST /api/contacts`)

Update contact (`PUT /api/contacts/:id`)

Delete contact (`DELETE /api/contacts/:id`)

This is a perfect use case for an API-only Phoenix app. You avoid unnecessary complexity and ship only the parts your mobile client needs.

The entire lifecycle—from writing controllers, to testing endpoints, to deploying your app—is simpler and more focused.

Phoenix API-only applications give you all the power of Phoenix without the overhead of rendering HTML or managing frontend assets. They're ideal for modern software stacks where the backend and frontend are decoupled. By using Phoenix's generators, JSON pipelines, and plug ecosystem, you can build secure, efficient, and production-ready APIs that are easy to scale and maintain.

Chapter 13: Full Project: Real-Time Collaboration Platform

In this chapter, we'll build a real-time collaboration platform from scratch using Elixir and Phoenix. This chapter ties together everything you've learned so far—contexts, channels, LiveView, background jobs, authentication, and deployment. We'll walk step-by-step through designing a scalable architecture, implementing real-time collaborative features, and preparing the application for production deployment.

Designing the Application Architecture

Before you write any code, it's critical to have a clearly defined architectural structure for your application. You're not just building features; you're shaping a system that needs to be scalable, concurrent, reliable, and easy to maintain. For a real-time collaboration platform, you're dealing with multiple users interacting with the same data at the same time, and that requires thoughtful coordination of backend services, data flows, and state management.

To approach this systematically, start by mapping your requirements into modules and responsibilities that align with Phoenix's strengths. Each feature—authentication, live editing, notifications, background jobs—must be planned as part of a cohesive architecture, not tacked on as an afterthought.

Identifying Functional Domains

The first thing you should do is break your application down into clear domains. In Phoenix, it's best to structure your project around *contexts*. A context encapsulates business logic and acts as the boundary between your external interfaces (controllers, LiveViews, APIs) and your internal data operations.

For a collaboration platform, the main areas of concern are:

Managing users and sessions (authentication and access control)

Creating and editing documents (collaboration engine)

Tracking who is online and active (presence system)

Sending real-time updates across clients (sockets and PubSub)

Delivering notifications (both in-app and external like emails)

Scheduling and running background tasks (with job queues)

Scaling and distributing workloads across nodes (clustering support)

These areas can be mapped into the following Elixir contexts:

`Accounts` – handles users, sessions, and access policies.

`Collaboration` – manages documents and synchronization logic.

`Presence` – tracks connected users, who is online, and where.

`Notifications` – queues and displays alerts or reminders.

`Background` – runs asynchronous tasks like emailing or document cleanup.

Each context should own its data schemas, changesets, queries, and commands.

Designing Document Collaboration Logic

At the core of the system is real-time document editing. Each document has an owner, possibly multiple editors, a revision history, and a synchronized state that is actively shared between connected clients.

You'll use Phoenix LiveView to handle the dynamic user interface and Phoenix Channels to manage the underlying real-time synchronization between users. Each document needs to be tracked by a process (either transient or persistent) that can manage its current state in memory and synchronize updates with the database as needed.

Here's a basic schema for a collaborative document:

```
defmodule MyApp.Collaboration.Document do
  use Ecto.Schema
  import Ecto.Changeset

  schema "documents" do
    field :title, :string
    field :body, :string
```

```
    belongs_to :owner, MyApp.Accounts.User

    timestamps()
  end

  def changeset(document, attrs) do
    document
    |> cast(attrs, [:title, :body, :owner_id])
    |> validate_required([:title, :body,
:owner_id])
  end
end
```

This schema defines the editable state of a document. For live collaboration, each change to the body will need to be broadcast in real time, persisted efficiently, and reflected in the user interface with minimal delay.

Planning Real-Time Communication

Every user connected to a document needs to receive updates as they happen. This requires efficient use of Phoenix PubSub and channels. Clients subscribe to a topic like `document:<id>`, and whenever a change is made, it's broadcast to that topic.

For this to scale across nodes in production, your app must support distributed PubSub through clustering. That means your Phoenix application must be aware of other nodes, and Phoenix.PubSub should propagate updates across them.

Here's a basic topic structure and PubSub usage:

```
topic = "document:#{document.id}"

Phoenix.PubSub.broadcast(MyApp.PubSub, topic,
%{event: "updated", body: new_body})
```

Connected clients react to this payload and update their interfaces accordingly.

Tracking Presence and User State

It's important for users to know who else is editing a document. Phoenix Presence helps track this without needing a custom solution.

When users join a LiveView or channel for a document, they're tracked by Presence under that document's topic. Their metadata—like username or cursor position—can also be stored and shared.

Here's an example of tracking presence in a channel:

```
Presence.track(socket, socket.assigns.user_id, %{

  username: socket.assigns.current_user.username,

  online_at: System.system_time(:second)

})
```

This data becomes available to all connected clients and can be rendered in the UI, creating a sense of shared activity.

Handling Notifications and Background Jobs

Collaboration often generates side effects—someone edits a shared document, and others need to be notified. Notifications can be queued in your database and optionally sent via email. Emailing is a non-blocking operation and should never be done in the request cycle.

For jobs like these, use Oban, a robust Elixir job processing library. It runs on Ecto/Postgres and supports retries, scheduled jobs, and worker queues.

When a document is edited, you can queue a job like this:

```
Oban.insert!(MyApp.Workers.EmailNotifier.new(%{

  user_id: collaborator.id,

  message: "Document #{doc.title} was just
updated."

}))
```

Oban takes care of executing this job in the background, without blocking the user's interaction.

Preparing for Distribution and Clustering

In production, your app will likely run on multiple nodes for high availability. To support this, configure `libcluster` to enable node discovery and join nodes into a cluster.

That way, when a user updates a document on Node A, and another user is connected on Node B, the event will still be broadcast through PubSub and received instantly.

Add the library:

```
{:libcluster, "~> 3.3"}
```

Configure clustering with a strategy like gossip in your config:

```
config :libcluster,

  topologies: [

    my_app_cluster: [

      strategy: Cluster.Strategy.Gossip

    ]

  ]
```

Clustering ensures your real-time and presence features work reliably across all application instances.

The architecture you design must be modular, predictable, and built around Phoenix's strengths. Each context is responsible for a bounded area of logic and storage. Real-time behavior is handled through LiveView, Channels, and PubSub. Side effects and notifications are delegated to background workers. And the system is capable of scaling horizontally through clustering.

This structure is not hypothetical. It's the kind of architecture used in production-grade collaboration platforms built with Phoenix today. It enables low-latency interactions, reliable messaging, resilient data updates, and a real-time experience that scales under load.

Building Core Features: Authentication, Collaboration, Notifications

Once the architecture is established, the next step is to implement the critical features that drive your application's functionality. These include user authentication, collaborative document handling, and real-time and asynchronous notifications. These features work together to ensure that users can access the system securely, collaborate on shared content seamlessly, and receive timely feedback about activities that affect them.

Authentication: Secure Access and User Identity

User authentication is foundational. Phoenix provides a first-party generator that handles registration, login, session management, and password hashing with security best practices in mind.

To scaffold authentication, use the `phx.gen.auth` task:

```
mix phx.gen.auth Accounts User users
```

This command creates:

A `User` schema with hashed passwords

An `Accounts` context for user management

Templates and controllers for registration, session, and confirmation

Middleware plugs to secure routes

After generating the auth system, apply the required database changes:

```
mix ecto.migrate
```

Now, update your router to include the auth routes:

```
# lib/my_app_web/router.ex
scope "/", MyAppWeb do
  pipe_through [:browser,
:require_authenticated_user]

  live "/documents", DocumentLive.Index
  live "/documents/:id", DocumentLive.Show
```

```
end                                                          |
```

For API-only projects, replace browser sessions with token-based authentication using libraries like Guardian or PowAssent for OAuth.

To enforce authentication in a controller or LiveView:

```
plug :require_authenticated_user                             |
```

In LiveView:

```
@impl true
def mount(_params, session, socket) do
  case session["user_token"] do
    nil -> {:halt, redirect(socket, to:
"/users/log_in")}
    _ -> {:ok, assign(socket, :current_user,
get_user_from_token(session["user_token"]))}
  end
end
```

With the authentication system in place, you now have secure endpoints that only logged-in users can access, each user is uniquely identified, and user-related permissions can be enforced consistently across the application.

Collaboration: Document Management and Real-Time Editing

At the core of the platform is a document system where users can collaborate. Start by generating the document schema:

```
mix phx.gen.context Collaboration Document
documents title:string body:text
user_id:references:users

mix ecto.migrate
```

The generated files include:

A Document schema

A Collaboration context

Functions like list_documents, get_document!, create_document, and update_document

Here's the core of the document schema:

```elixir
defmodule MyApp.Collaboration.Document do
  use Ecto.Schema
  import Ecto.Changeset

  schema "documents" do
    field :title, :string
    field :body, :string
    belongs_to :user, MyApp.Accounts.User

    timestamps()
  end

  def changeset(document, attrs) do
    document
    |> cast(attrs, [:title, :body, :user_id])
    |> validate_required([:title, :body, :user_id])
  end
end
```

To allow users to view and edit documents in real time, create a LiveView for DocumentLive.Show.

```elixir
defmodule MyAppWeb.DocumentLive.Show do
  use MyAppWeb, :live_view

  alias MyApp.Collaboration

  @impl true
  def mount(%{"id" => id}, _session, socket) do
    document = Collaboration.get_document!(id)
    {:ok, assign(socket, document: document, body:
document.body)}
  end

  @impl true
  def handle_event("edit", %{"body" => new_body},
socket) do
    document = socket.assigns.document
    {:ok, updated} =
Collaboration.update_document(document, %{body:
new_body})
```

273

```
      {:noreply, assign(socket, body: updated.body)}
   end
end
```

Now you have a dynamic UI where users can see and modify documents in real time. You can later integrate Channels and PubSub to allow simultaneous edits across users and connected clients.

Notifications: Keeping Users Informed

Collaboration is not just about writing together—it also involves awareness of changes. Users should be notified when someone edits a shared document, comments on it, or sends them a message.

Create a Notification schema:

```
mix phx.gen.schema Notifications.Notification
notifications user_id:references:users
message:string read:boolean

mix ecto.migrate
```

Inside the Notifications context, define a function to send a notification:

```
defmodule MyApp.Notifications do

   alias MyApp.Repo

   alias MyApp.Notifications.Notification


   def notify_user(user_id, message) do

     %Notification{}

     |> Notification.changeset(%{user_id: user_id,
message: message, read: false})

     |> Repo.insert()

   end

end
```

The changeset is straightforward:

```
def changeset(notification, attrs) do
  notification
  |> cast(attrs, [:user_id, :message, :read])
  |> validate_required([:user_id, :message])
end
```

This allows you to queue in-app alerts whenever something relevant happens. For example, after updating a document, notify all collaborators except the one who made the change:

```
Enum.each(collaborators, fn user ->
  if user.id != editor.id do
    Notifications.notify_user(user.id,
"#{editor.name} updated #{doc.title}")
  end
end)
```

These notifications can then be displayed in a dropdown or badge on the frontend. You can also extend this to support push notifications or emails, which will be handled in the next section using background jobs.

Putting It Together: Authenticated Collaboration with Feedback

Let's walk through how it works in context:

A user logs in via the Phoenix-generated auth system.

They open a document, triggering a LiveView mount and fetching the latest content.

As they edit, the document is updated in the database and the UI is refreshed.

Notifications are queued for other users involved with the document.

The system responds quickly, with clean separation of logic: authentication handled by `Accounts`, editing logic by `Collaboration`, and updates managed by `Notifications`.

Each layer is independent and testable, with clear data flow and responsibility boundaries.

Implementing Real-Time Editing with LiveView and Channels

When users are collaborating on a shared document, the editing experience must feel immediate and synchronized. Each participant should be able to see changes as they happen—without needing to refresh the page or reload the content. This is the kind of interactivity Phoenix was built for. LiveView and Channels together give you both the reactive frontend behavior and low-latency data transport necessary for implementing real-time document editing.

LiveView provides stateful components rendered over WebSockets. It's responsible for rendering the UI, reacting to input, and updating the page without client-side JavaScript. Channels, on the other hand, let you establish a persistent connection between clients so that updates made by one user can be broadcast to others.

To build collaborative editing, you'll use LiveView to handle the interface and Channels to handle cross-client synchronization.

Wiring the Document Interface with LiveView

Start by creating a LiveView module that renders the document editor. This view should allow a user to open a specific document, display its current contents, and listen for local edits.

Here's how the LiveView module is structured:

```
defmodule MyAppWeb.DocumentLive.Show do
  use MyAppWeb, :live_view

  alias MyApp.Collaboration
  alias MyAppWeb.Presence

  @topic_prefix "document"
```

```elixir
  @impl true
  def mount(%{"id" => id}, _session, socket) do
    if connected?(socket) do
      Phoenix.PubSub.subscribe(MyApp.PubSub,
topic(id))
      Presence.track(self(), topic(id), socket.id,
%{})
    end

    document = Collaboration.get_document!(id)

    {:ok,
     assign(socket,
       document: document,
       body: document.body,
       topic: topic(id),
       user_id: socket.id
     )}
  end

  @impl true
  def handle_event("edit", %{"body" => new_body},
socket) do
    {:ok, _updated} =
Collaboration.update_document(socket.assigns.docume
nt, %{body: new_body})
    Phoenix.PubSub.broadcast(MyApp.PubSub,
socket.assigns.topic, {:update_body, new_body})
    {:noreply, assign(socket, body: new_body)}
  end

  @impl true
  def handle_info({:update_body, new_body}, socket)
do
    {:noreply, assign(socket, body: new_body)}
  end

  defp topic(id), do: "#{@topic_prefix}:#{id}"
end
```

This mount function:

Fetches the document by ID

Subscribes the socket process to a PubSub topic (`document:<id>`)

Tracks user presence on the document

Initializes the LiveView state with the document body

When the user types and triggers the `"edit"` event, the new body is saved to the database, then broadcast to all subscribers of the document topic using `Phoenix.PubSub`.

Other clients receive the update via the `handle_info/2` callback and update their local state.

This pattern ensures low-latency collaboration without building a full CRDT or operational transformation engine—ideal for cases where last-write-wins conflict resolution is acceptable.

Designing the Editable Interface

The template for this LiveView might look like this:

```
<form phx-change="edit">

  <textarea name="body" rows="20" cols="80" phx-hook="AutoFocus">

    <%= @body %>

  </textarea>

</form>
```

This form uses `phx-change` to send updates as the user types (you can throttle it with debouncing if needed). The `AutoFocus` hook is optional and helps maintain editing focus when the DOM re-renders.

You can enhance this with collaborative cursors or inline highlights using more advanced LiveView JS hooks or by integrating client-side state (if needed).

Handling Broadcast Collisions and Optimization

When multiple users edit the same document at the same time, it's possible to encounter race conditions or overwrite changes. While this example assumes last-write-wins semantics (each update overwrites the body), you can easily integrate more advanced handling using diff patches or version tokens.

To avoid broadcasting an update to the sender itself (which can create UI jitter), use `broadcast_from/4`:

```
Phoenix.PubSub.broadcast_from(self(), MyApp.PubSub,
socket.assigns.topic, {:update_body, new_body})
```

This excludes the current process (which already has the new state), reducing unnecessary UI updates.

Augmenting Collaboration with Channels

LiveView gives you an excellent interface and server-side state, but when you're implementing advanced multi-user editing—such as collaborative cursors, simultaneous paragraph updates, or contextual chat—you need more granular control over user interactions. Channels are better suited for this because they allow bi-directional event dispatching between clients and the server outside the standard LiveView lifecycle.

Here's how you'd define a document channel:

```
defmodule MyAppWeb.DocumentChannel do
  use MyAppWeb, :channel

  def join("document:" <> doc_id, _params, socket)
do
    {:ok, assign(socket, :doc_id, doc_id)}
  end

  def handle_in("edit", %{"body" => new_body},
socket) do
    broadcast!(socket, "update", %{"body" =>
new_body})
    {:noreply, socket}
  end
end
```

And your client-side JavaScript might look like:

```
let socket = new Phoenix.Socket("/socket", {params:
{token: userToken}});
socket.connect();

let channel = socket.channel("document:" +
documentId, {});
channel.join();

channel.on("update", payload => {
  document.querySelector("textarea").value =
payload.body;
});

document.querySelector("textarea").addEventListener
("input", e => {
  channel.push("edit", {body: e.target.value});
});
```

This creates a real-time event pipeline from one user's typing to every other user's screen.

While LiveView can handle most editing scenarios, using Channels alongside LiveView is a powerful pattern when you want to separate interactive interface logic from real-time event coordination.

Tracking User Presence

Presence lets collaborators see who else is editing the document. Add this into your LiveView or Channel module:

```
MyAppWeb.Presence.track(
  self(),
  "document:#{document.id}",
  user_id,
  %{username: user.name, typing: false}
)
```

And retrieve the presence list with:

```
MyAppWeb.Presence.list("document:#{document.id}")
```

This gives you live data about who's connected. You can use it to show avatars, highlight collaborators, or even display who's currently typing.

LiveView excels at rendering the primary UI and handling local input efficiently. Channels give you the ability to push custom events across clients. The hybrid approach lets you:

Render and manage the editing interface with LiveView

Use Channels for granular, low-latency events like cursor sync, focus tracking, or typing notifications

Keep everything real-time without any polling

The two tools share a common transport (WebSockets), so they work together without interference.

Real-time editing in Phoenix is not an afterthought—it's a first-class pattern. Using LiveView and Channels in tandem, you can deliver an experience where users collaborate with minimal lag, no page refreshes, and reliable state synchronization. You've now built an interface that responds to every keystroke, synchronizes across users instantly, and is backed by a robust PubSub system that scales horizontally.

Background Jobs, Scaling, and Deployment

Once your application supports real-time interaction, collaborative editing, and user authentication, it's time to address essential system concerns: how to handle long-running or async tasks, how to scale across nodes, and how to prepare and deploy the application to production environments. These are not optional. Without proper background job handling or scalability planning, the application becomes brittle under load or fails to deliver messages, emails, or updates reliably.

Running Background Jobs with Oban

You should never handle time-consuming or failure-prone operations like email delivery, report generation, or external HTTP calls in the request/response cycle. These should be delegated to job queues. In the Elixir ecosystem, Oban is the most reliable option. It's built on Ecto and PostgreSQL, supports retries, scheduling, prioritization, and is backed by a robust plugin system.

Start by adding Oban to your `mix.exs`:

```
defp deps do

  [

    {:oban, "~> 2.15"}

  ]

end
```

Install dependencies:

```
mix deps.get
```

Then configure Oban in your `config/config.exs`:

```
config :my_app, Oban,

  repo: MyApp.Repo,

  plugins: [Oban.Plugins.Pruner],

  queues: [default: 10, mailers: 5]
```

This sets up two queues (`default` and `mailers`) with worker concurrency limits.

Run the required migration:

```
mix oban.migrations
```

```
mix ecto.migrate
```

Next, define a worker. This is a module that receives job arguments and executes logic.

```
defmodule MyApp.Workers.EmailNotifier do
  use Oban.Worker

  alias MyApp.Mailer
  alias MyApp.Accounts

  @impl Oban.Worker
```

```
  def perform(%Oban.Job{args: %{"user_id" =>
user_id, "message" => message}}) do
    user = Accounts.get_user!(user_id)
    email =
MyApp.Emails.build_notification_email(user.email,
message)
    Mailer.deliver_now(email)
    :ok
  end
end
```

Now queue the job anywhere in your app logic:

```
%{user_id: user.id, message: "Your document was
updated."}

|> MyApp.Workers.EmailNotifier.new()

|> Oban.insert()
```

This inserts a job into the database. A supervised Oban process polls for jobs and executes them within your application's supervision tree.

If the email server fails, the job will retry automatically based on exponential backoff.

You can also schedule jobs:

```
MyApp.Workers.EmailNotifier.new(%{user_id: id,
message: msg}, schedule_in: 600)
```

This queues the job to run 10 minutes from now.

Oban includes a Web UI as a separate package (oban_web) if you want to visually monitor job execution.

Scaling with Clustering and Distributed PubSub

When running your application on multiple nodes (for example, in a production deployment across multiple machines or containers), you need to ensure real-time features like Phoenix PubSub and Presence continue to work correctly across those nodes.

Phoenix PubSub supports distributed communication, but it depends on node discovery. This is where `libcluster` comes in.

First, add it to your dependencies:

```
{:libcluster, "~> 3.3"}
```

Then configure a topology in `config/runtime.exs` or `config.exs` depending on your deployment environment:

```
config :libcluster,
  topologies: [
    my_app_cluster: [
      strategy: Cluster.Strategy.Gossip,
      config: [
        port: 45892
      ]
    ]
  ]
```

This uses the gossip strategy, which works well in environments like Fly.io or Kubernetes, where each node can discover others through peer metadata.

Start the cluster supervisor in your application:

```
# lib/my_app/application.ex
children = [
  {Cluster.Supervisor,
[Application.get_env(:libcluster, :topologies),
[name: MyApp.ClusterSupervisor]]}
]
```

Once this is running, messages broadcasted on one node (e.g. `Phoenix.PubSub.broadcast/3`) will reach subscribers on other nodes. Presence tracking will also work globally.

This is critical for real-time collaboration: when two users are connected to two different nodes, your system must guarantee that updates flow between them in real-time. Without clustering, they will be isolated.

Building and Deploying Phoenix Releases

Phoenix supports building OTP releases using Elixir's `mix release` system. This produces a fully self-contained binary you can run in production with no need for Elixir installed on the server.

First, add `runtime.exs` configuration if you need to load secrets at runtime:

```
# config/runtime.exs

config :my_app, MyAppWeb.Endpoint,

  url: [host: System.get_env("PHX_HOST"), port:
443],

  secret_key_base:
System.fetch_env!("SECRET_KEY_BASE"),

  server: true
```

Then generate a release:

```
MIX_ENV=prod mix release
```

The compiled release lives in `_build/prod/rel/my_app`. Start it with:

```
_build/prod/rel/my_app/bin/my_app start
```

To deploy, you can copy the release to any Linux host and run it as a service. You can also containerize it using Docker, or deploy to platforms like:

Fly.io – great for clustering and easy deployment

Render – ideal for smaller apps with managed databases

Gigalixir – PaaS designed for Elixir apps

Fly.io example deployment with clustering:

```
flyctl launch
```

Fly automatically configures node discovery via private networking and supports stateful clustering out of the box.

Production Tips and Observability

Enable telemetry and metrics using tools like:

285

PromEx – for detailed metrics and Grafana dashboards

Sentry – for error tracking

AppSignal – for full-stack performance insights

Add this to your supervision tree to observe system behavior in production:

```
Telemetry.attach("oban-success", [:oban, :job,
:stop], fn event, measurements, metadata, _ ->

  IO.inspect({event, measurements, metadata})

end, nil)
```

You'll also want to make use of Phoenix's built-in request logger, structured logging with `LoggerJSON`, and job execution metrics via Oban.

By integrating Oban, you ensure long-running and external operations are reliable, retryable, and offloaded from your user flows. With clustering configured, your app supports distributed presence, PubSub, and LiveView updates across horizontally scaled nodes. And with releases, your application becomes portable, secure, and production-ready.

Appendices

Appendix A: Advanced BEAM Concepts

The BEAM (Bogdan/Björn's Erlang Abstract Machine) is the virtual machine that runs all Elixir and Erlang applications. It is designed for concurrency, fault tolerance, and soft real-time systems. While most Phoenix developers rarely need to interact with the BEAM directly, understanding some of its advanced features can help you build more reliable and high-performance systems. This appendix introduces three such features: hot code upgrades, ETS (Erlang Term Storage), and Native Implemented Functions (NIFs).

Hot Code Upgrades

A *hot code upgrade* is the ability to change a running system's code without shutting it down or dropping user connections. This feature is built into the BEAM and is one of the reasons why Erlang has been widely used in telecom and financial systems that require high availability.

How It Works

Each module in Elixir or Erlang can have two versions loaded at the same time: the *current* and the *old*. When you upgrade a module, the current version becomes old, and the new version takes its place. The BEAM ensures that running processes finish their work with the old version before fully switching over.

Using Releases and `:release_handler`

Hot upgrades require you to use OTP releases, typically built with `mix release`. You generate upgrade instructions using tools like `:release_handler` and `.appup` files.

Example upgrade flow:

You build a new release.

You generate a `.appup` file describing how to upgrade.

You deploy the new version alongside the running system.

You instruct the BEAM to apply the upgrade in-place.

While powerful, hot upgrades are complex and error-prone. You need to manage state transitions carefully, especially when changing data structures. For this reason, many teams prefer rolling restarts with clustering instead of true hot upgrades.

When to Use

Use hot code upgrades when you're running distributed nodes that must remain available and cannot afford downtime—even for seconds. In practice, most Phoenix applications use blue/green or canary deployments instead.

ETS Tables and In-Memory Storage

ETS (Erlang Term Storage) is an in-memory key-value storage system built into the BEAM. It allows storing large amounts of data in memory, accessible from any process, with support for concurrent reads and writes.

Creating and Using ETS Tables

ETS tables are typically created using the `:ets.new/2` function:

```
table = :ets.new(:session_cache, [:set, :public,
:named_table])
```

Here's what each option means:

`:set` — unique keys, like a map.

`:public` — any process can read/write.

`:named_table` — accessible by name instead of reference.

You can insert and look up values like this:

```
:ets.insert(:session_cache, {:user_1, %{status:
:online}})
:ets.lookup(:session_cache, :user_1)
```

This gives you a lightweight, process-independent cache or registry.

ETS Characteristics

Fast and built into the BEAM runtime.

Not garbage-collected like process memory.

Data is not persisted—restarts clear it.

Supports select queries, match specs, and concurrent access.

ETS is great for building things like:

Caches for API responses.

Session and presence registries.

Temporary lookup tables or counters.

Managing Table Ownership

ETS tables are owned by a process. When the owning process dies, the table is destroyed. To avoid accidental loss, many applications create ETS tables under supervised GenServers or long-lived processes.

```
defmodule MyApp.ETSManager do
  use GenServer

  def start_link(_) do
    GenServer.start_link(__MODULE__, :ok, name:
__MODULE__)
  end

  @impl true
  def init(:ok) do
    :ets.new(:session_cache, [:named_table,
:public, :set])
    {:ok, %{}}
  end
end
```

Native Implemented Functions (NIFs)

NIFs allow you to write performance-critical code in native languages like C or Rust and call it directly from Elixir or Erlang. This is useful when certain algorithms or operations are too slow in pure Elixir, such as heavy numerical computations, cryptographic operations, or encoding/decoding binary formats.

How NIFs Work

When you write a NIF, you create a shared library that is loaded into the BEAM's address space. This allows Elixir code to invoke native code as if it were a regular function.

Example (simplified C NIF):

```
static ERL_NIF_TERM add(ErlNifEnv* env, int argc,
const ERL_NIF_TERM argv[]) {
  int a, b;
  enif_get_int(env, argv[0], &a);
  enif_get_int(env, argv[1], &b);
  return enif_make_int(env, a + b);
}
```

Then in Elixir:

```
defmodule MyMath do
  use Rustler, otp_app: :my_app, crate: "mymath"

  def add(_a, _b), do:
:erlang.nif_error(:nif_not_loaded)
end
```

Libraries like Rustler make it easier to write NIFs in Rust and integrate them safely into your application.

Risks and Considerations

NIFs run in the same OS thread as the BEAM scheduler. If they block or crash, they can bring down the whole VM. To avoid this:

Keep NIFs short and non-blocking.

Use Dirty NIFs (marked as CPU or IO-bound) for longer tasks.

Carefully test memory safety and input validation.

Unless you truly need low-level performance, prefer Elixir for safety and maintainability.

Appendix B: Recommended Libraries and Tools

The Elixir and Phoenix ecosystem continues to grow with libraries and tools that support development, observability, performance, and user experience. While Phoenix itself provides powerful foundations, several community-driven projects extend its capabilities significantly. This appendix introduces key libraries that are well-supported, production-tested, and highly useful across a variety of applications—from frontend UI components to streaming data pipelines and native application interfaces.

Surface

Surface is a component-based UI library built on top of Phoenix LiveView. It introduces a declarative syntax similar to Vue or React, with compile-time validation, strong props and slot handling, and better encapsulation.

Instead of raw HTML and heex, Surface provides a structured and maintainable way to define LiveView components:

```
defmodule MyAppWeb.Components.Alert do
  use Surface.Component

  prop type, :string, default: "info"
  slot default

  def render(assigns) do
    ~F"""
    <div class={"alert alert-#{@type}"}>
      <#slot />
    </div>
    """
  end
end
```

Surface improves developer productivity, makes LiveView code more reusable, and introduces patterns that are more familiar to frontend developers with experience in component-based frameworks.

Surface works with Tailwind CSS, Bootstrap, or custom styles, and supports slot-based composition and form bindings.

Broadway

Broadway is a data ingestion and processing framework built by the team at Dashbit. It provides a structured and concurrent way to consume large volumes of external data using producers like RabbitMQ, Kafka, or AWS SQS, and process that data through pipelines with backpressure, batching, retries, and metrics.

A basic Broadway pipeline might look like this:

```
defmodule MyApp.Consumers.EmailPipeline do
  use Broadway

  alias Broadway.Message

  def start_link(_opts) do
    Broadway.start_link(__MODULE__,
      name: __MODULE__,
      producer: [module:
{BroadwayRabbitMQ.Producer, queue: "emails"}],
      processors: [default: [concurrency: 10]],
      batchers: [email: [batch_size: 20,
batch_timeout: 100]]
    )
  end

  def handle_message(_, %Message{data: payload} =
message, _) do
    process_email(payload)
    Message.ack_immediately(message)
  end
end
```

Broadway is a great choice when your application needs to process event streams, transactional events, or heavy background workloads from queues.

Scenic

Scenic is a UI framework for building **graphical interfaces** in native Elixir using Nerves and OpenGL. It's primarily used in embedded systems, kiosks, and hardware devices that require GUIs directly on physical screens.

Unlike LiveView, which targets browsers, Scenic renders directly to hardware or desktop surfaces. You define scenes using declarative components like buttons, graphs, and layouts:

```
graph
```

```
|> text("Welcome", translate: {20, 40})

|> button("Start", id: :start_button, translate: {20, 80})
```

Scenic integrates well with Nerves and supports touchscreen interactions and animation. It is not designed for browser-based applications, but it fills a niche where you need Elixir-powered graphical interfaces running on Raspberry Pi, industrial hardware, or custom display setups.

LiveView Native

LiveView Native is an evolving effort to bridge Phoenix LiveView with native mobile user interfaces. It allows a mobile client (e.g., iOS or Android) to connect to a LiveView server and render native UI components driven by LiveView diffs.

This enables you to write backend-driven native UIs with real-time updates, similar to how LiveView manages browser UIs.

Instead of HTML, LiveView Native communicates layout descriptions in a platform-specific DSL (such as SwiftUI) over the wire.

Example (Swift LiveView Native template):

```
<Stack>

  <Text>Welcome</Text>

  <Button phx-click="register">Get Started</Button>

</Stack>
```

This is still in active development, but it opens the door for Elixir developers to build native apps without writing traditional mobile client logic. It's particularly attractive for teams building custom clients for controlled environments like kiosks or vertical SaaS platforms.

Helpful Packages for Development and Production

Oban

Oban is a background job processing system built on top of PostgreSQL. It's used for handling tasks like emails, retries, queueing, and scheduled jobs.

Supports multiple queues, workers, delays, priorities, and error handling

Integrates with Telemetry for observability

Offers a Web UI (via `oban_web`) for managing jobs

Swoosh + Mailer

Swoosh is an email library that works with various adapters such as SMTP, SendGrid, or Amazon SES. Combined with Phoenix's built-in `Mailer` module, it's a simple way to add email support to any app.

ExUnit + Wallaby

For testing, `ExUnit` is built-in, but `Wallaby` helps with end-to-end browser testing. It's especially useful for LiveView interfaces where you need to simulate clicks, form submissions, and DOM updates.

Telemetry + PromEx

Telemetry is the foundation for metrics and observability in Phoenix. `PromEx` builds on this to expose metrics in Prometheus format and even provides out-of-the-box Grafana dashboards.

libcluster + Horde

`libcluster` handles automatic node discovery for distributed apps.

`Horde` allows distributed supervisors and registries so that processes can be balanced and failover across nodes.

Bandit

Bandit is a drop-in HTTP server replacement for Cowboy, written in Elixir. It's designed to integrate more cleanly with Plug and supports HTTP/2 and future Phoenix enhancements.

The Elixir ecosystem offers robust, actively maintained libraries that can support web, mobile, IoT, background processing, and high-concurrency workloads. Whether you're building traditional Phoenix apps, background job systems, real-time UIs, or native device interfaces, these tools enable professional-grade performance and maintainability without needing external languages or fragile integrations.

Appendix C: Resources for Further Learning

Learning Elixir and Phoenix doesn't end with a book or course. The ecosystem continues to grow, and staying productive means knowing where to find reliable references, active communities, and high-quality open source examples. This appendix lists trusted documentation, learning materials, and community-driven projects that can help you deepen your knowledge, adopt best practices, and stay current with improvements in the platform.

Official Documentation

The official documentation for Elixir and Phoenix is well-written, regularly updated, and highly recommended as a primary source of truth. It includes reference material, tutorials, and API specifications.

Elixir Core Documentation

Main site: https://elixir-lang.org

Docs: https://hexdocs.pm/elixir

You'll find:

Language reference for modules like `Enum`, `Map`, `Task`, `GenServer`

Guides on concurrency, processes, and metaprogramming

Mix and compilation tools documentation

Phoenix Framework

Main site: https://phoenixframework.org

Docs: https://hexdocs.pm/phoenix

Covers:

LiveView usage and lifecycle

Router, controllers, views, and channels

Testing and deployment guides

HexDocs

Index of all Hex packages: https://hexdocs.pm

HexDocs hosts documentation for nearly every Elixir library published to Hex, including Oban, Ecto, Broadway, Absinthe, Swoosh, and more. Use it to check APIs, versions, and guides for any dependency.

Books, Blogs, and Community Resources

While official docs are useful for reference, books and blog posts help provide deeper explanations, guided examples, and best practices.

Books

Programming Elixir (Dave Thomas) – Covers the language thoroughly, from basics to OTP.

Elixir in Action (Saša Jurić) – Emphasizes building concurrent, fault-tolerant systems.

Programming Phoenix LiveView (Pragmatic Bookshelf) – Focuses on building real-time web interfaces with LiveView.

Designing Elixir Systems with OTP (Pragmatic Bookshelf) – Teaches how to structure maintainable, scalable OTP applications.

Blogs and Publications

The Dashbit Blog: https://dashbit.co/blog
High-quality posts by the creators of Elixir and LiveView, covering design decisions, performance tips, and library updates.

Fly.io Blog: https://fly.io/phoenix-files
Excellent articles on deploying and scaling Phoenix apps, clustering, and working with real-time features.

Plataformatec Archive: Many foundational Elixir articles are archived at https://blog.plataformatec.com.br.

Elixir Radar: A free weekly newsletter that shares tutorials, announcements, and library releases.

Open Source Projects to Study

Studying real-world open source projects can reveal how seasoned developers structure applications, handle edge cases, and use Phoenix and OTP idiomatically.

Hex.pm

Source: https://github.com/hexpm/hexpm

The actual codebase behind Hex.pm, the Elixir package manager. Shows real use of Phoenix, API structure, Ecto, background jobs, and tests.

Changelog.com

Source: https://github.com/thechangelog/changelog.com

A production-grade Phoenix web app with audio streaming, authentication, background processing, and webhooks.

Pleroma

Source: https://git.pleroma.social/pleroma/pleroma

A federated social network server written in Elixir. Useful for understanding multi-user, distributed apps with large state and real-time communication.

Oban

Source: https://github.com/sorentwo/oban

Even if you're not contributing, reading the Oban code can help you understand how supervised background workers and job queues are designed using GenServer, telemetry, and pub/sub.

Community Platforms

The Elixir community is supportive and technically focused. There are several active spaces where you can ask questions, discuss libraries, and learn from other developers.

Elixir Forum: https://elixirforum.com
The main discussion forum. Great for getting help and seeing what others are building.

Elixir Slack: https://elixir-slackin.herokuapp.com
A real-time chat community with active channels for Phoenix, LiveView, Nerves, Absinthe, and more.

Discord: https://discord.gg/elixir
An alternative to Slack with open voice channels and active discussion.

GitHub Discussions and Issues: For popular projects like Phoenix, LiveView, and Ecto, many technical discussions happen directly on GitHub.

Whether you're just starting out or building production systems with Elixir and Phoenix, having reliable references and exposure to high-quality code is essential. The official documentation, active community platforms, and production-grade open source projects in the Elixir ecosystem make continuous learning accessible and practical. By staying connected to these resources, you'll keep your skills sharp and your projects aligned with best practices.